Motivation to Learn

Classroom Insights from Educational Psychology Series

Motivation to Learn

Transforming Classroom Culture to Support Student Achievement

Michael Middleton

Kevin Perks

A Joint Publication

CORWIN
A SAGE Company

FOR INFORMATION:

Corwin

A SAGE Company

2455 Teller Road

Thousand Oaks, California 91320

(800) 233-9936

www.corwin.com

SAGE Publications Ltd.

1 Oliver's Yard

55 City Road

London EC1Y 1SP

United Kingdom

SAGE Publications India Pvt. Ltd.

B 1/I 1 Mohan Cooperative Industrial Area

Mathura Road, New Delhi 110 044

India

SAGE Publications Asia-Pacific Pte. Ltd.

3 Church Street

#10-04 Samsung Hub

Singapore 049483

Printed in the United States of America

A catalog record of this book may be found in the Library of Congress.

ISBN 978-1-4129-8671-7

This book is printed on acid-free paper.

Acquisitions Editor: Jessica Allan

Associate Editor: Kimberly Greenberg

Editorial Assistant: Cesar Reyes

Production Editor: Amy Schroller

Copy Editor: Codi Bowman

Typesetter: C&M Digitals (P) Ltd.

Proofreader: Sue Irwin

Indexer: Karen Wiley

Cover Designer: Candice Harman

MIX
Paper from
responsible sources
FSC® C014174

14 15 16 17 18 10 9 8 7 6 5 4 3 2 1

Contents

Publisher's Acknowledgments

Corwin gratefully acknowledges the contributions of the following reviewers:

Amie Brown
Teacher
Floyd County Schools
Rome, GA

Charla Buford Bunker
Literacy Specialist
Great Falls Public Schools
Sun River, MT

Margarete Couture
Elementary Principal
South Seneca Central School District
Interlaken, NY

Melanie Mares Sainz
Academic Coach
Lowndes Middle School
Valdosta, GA

Lauren Mittermann
Social Studies Teacher, Grades 7 and 8
Gibraltar Secondary School
Fish Creek, WI

About the Authors

 **Michael Middleton** is an associate professor and chair of the Education Department at the University of New Hampshire where he researches the relation of classroom and culture to adolescent identity and motivation in diverse community settings. Currently, he holds the John and H. Irene Peters Professorship in Education to support his teaching, research, and service and has been a recipient of a UNH Faculty Excellence in Teaching Award. Primarily, his teaching focuses on the preparation of educators to meet the complex demands of classroom teaching. Early in his career, Michael was a high school mathematics teacher working with at-risk youth. He currently lives in New Hampshire with his son.

 **Kevin Perks** is a program and research associate with WestEd who works with schools and districts across the country to support motivation, engagement, and achievement in such areas as standards-based education, literacy, and educational reform. Most recently, Kevin has been working with districts to support the implementation of the Common Core State Standards across all content areas. Kevin began his career in Ohio where he taught at a private school dedicated to addressing the needs of underserved learners with dyslexia and other learning disabilities. Since then he has taught a variety of subjects from K-12 to the university level. Kevin currently lives in Maine with his wife and daughter.

I am dedicating this work to my family and to the teachers and colleagues who have profoundly influenced my life. The memory of my parents has been the inspiration for me to overcome challenges and to serve our communities. My son Daniel, nieces Kate and Hannah, and nephew Harry teach me each day about love, learning, and motivation. Finally, my mentor and friend Carol Midgley was an inspiration for her tireless work on improving schools for all our children.

—MM

I would like to dedicate this book to the numerous teachers who helped me to find my own motivation, and to those willing to share their stories. In particular, I dedicate this book to Celia Millward, my daughter's namesake. To George Hillocks who nurtured my passion for teaching and learning early in my career. To my coauthor, mentor, and friend Mike who, even when I was a student of his, always treated me as a respected colleague. To my parents and my brothers who, since the day I was born, modeled a love of learning and the importance of hard work. To my colleagues at MSAD 60 who continue to challenge me to do my best, especially Kate and Heidi. To my wife Jessica, whose patience and kindness I strive (and often fail) to emulate. And finally to my daughter Celia, who teaches me more than I can ever hope to teach her. To quote singer/song-writer Lori McKenna, "I think it's fair to say kid, you taught me right."

—KP

SECTION I

Understanding Student Motivation

INTRODUCTION

THE NATURE OF MOTIVATION IN THE CLASSROOM

In our work as teachers and with teachers for more than two decades, few topics have been more prevalent in the discourse of teaching and learning than motivation. Motivation captures the imagination of veteran and novice teachers alike. It is an often sought—but less often found—quality of students and classrooms. In hallways, classrooms, and meeting places, we hear statements such as these:

"She's so motivated. That girl will go far."

"My class was involved and energetic today."

At times we also hear these:

"My fourth period class is a bunch of duds. They sit there and won't participate."

"He'd do well if he just applied himself. He's just not
motivated."

These comments and others like them attest to the puzzling
and elusive nature of motivation. Sometimes teaching and
learning feels magical. At other times, it can be arduous and
challenging. Our goal in this book is to make motivation less
elusive and to provide teachers with tools and ways of thinking
to make those magical moments a more common occurrence.

There has been an evolution of how motivation has been
conceptualized and understood over the past century. During
this time, cognitive and social scientists have engaged in a variety of research to better understand the nature of motivation.
This research has yielded valuable insights into what motivates
learners, including the complexity of motivational processes.
Early conceptions of motivation viewed it as an individual
drive that was a part of every person as a way to fulfill basic
needs. Conceptions of motivation then shifted to recognize
the important role our environment plays in shaping an individual's motivation. Some suggested that motivation occurred
as the individual responded to environmental stimuli. The next
generation of motivation research has used a person-in-context
approach and understood motivation as the result of individuals making sense of the environment and acting accordingly.
However, recently researchers have recognized that motivation
is even more dynamic and is shaped and influenced by the activity that takes place between individuals and their environment.
These overly simplified descriptions of motivation theories
imply that there are many variables that influence the motivation of an individual and the motivational climate in a classroom.

MOTIVATION AS A DYNAMIC SYSTEM

Despite the recognition that motivation is highly complex, our
increased understanding of motivation provides a wealth of
information about teaching practices that are more likely to
produce the type of learning environments that we all desire.
We know that teachers across all grade levels and disciplines

struggle on a daily basis to cultivate classroom environments marked by energetic, focused interactions with students that produce interest and thoughtfulness, where time seems to pass quickly, and high-quality work is produced. Our hope is that teachers will use this book to transform their classrooms and schools into contexts characterized by motivated students engaged in deep learning and to truly reflect on their practices as one tool for continual improvement.

Evolution of Motivation Theories

Motivation as an Individual Drive

Motivation as a Response to the Environment

Motivation as a Person-in-Context

Motivation as a Dynamic System

REFLECTIVE PRACTICE ACTIVITY

List two or three goals you have for reading this book.

1.

2.

3.

Why are you reading this book? Are you reading it as part of a class or professional learning community? How might your purpose for reading this book affect your motivation?

Are there others you could involve in a discussion of this book? If so, how? How does their participation influence your motivation?

Guiding Metaphors

Metaphors provide a powerful way to help teachers understand motivation in a way that can help shape teaching and learning. How teachers conceive motivation is likely to impact the way they view students, as well as the teaching and learning process. In our experience, two metaphors have dominated how educators think about motivation in the classroom: the metaphor of the gas tank and the metaphor of the garden.

Common Metaphors for Motivation

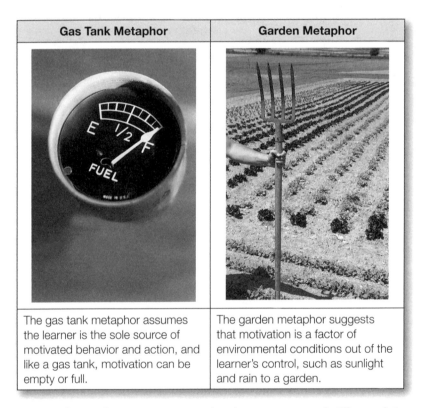

Gas Tank Metaphor	Garden Metaphor
The gas tank metaphor assumes the learner is the sole source of motivated behavior and action, and like a gas tank, motivation can be empty or full.	The garden metaphor suggests that motivation is a factor of environmental conditions out of the learner's control, such as sunlight and rain to a garden.

Teachers often compare motivation to a gas tank. The tank is either full or empty. This approach to understanding motivation assumes that motivation resides within each individual student

We propose that teaching and learning are much like rafting down a river. We urge teachers to view themselves as river guides attempting to guide a group of paddlers downstream. This may involve understanding the paddlers' level of readiness to lead them into rapids that are challenging but not dangerous for them. The river can be viewed as the curriculum that the learners seek to master; it may present unanticipated challenges, and lead to a promised but uncertain endpoint. The river, like a classroom, is the context in which all the work is situated. Motivation is represented by the currents that provide momentum and direction for progress along the journey. From this perspective, we encourage teachers to view motivation not as something that they supply, nor as something that is beyond their control. Instead, we urge readers to conceptualize **motivation as a dynamic, ever-present force** that may ebb and flow according to conditions, which learners may use to their advantage or choose to ignore, and that every teacher needs to "read" and understand to guide each learner. When properly harnessed, motivation, like a current, propels learning forward.

Motivation as a Current

The metaphor of motivation as a current reveals its ever-present, dynamic, and powerful nature.

The metaphor that motivation is like the current in a river works for a variety of reasons. First, it recognizes that without motivation we cannot meet our goals in a productive and efficient manner. Effective teachers recognize this and see themselves as guides who know how to navigate the waters of the curriculum with each student. They know how to read the motivational currents and how to use a variety of tools to help students harness this energy to reach their goals. Second, this metaphor recognizes that motivation in the classroom is dynamic—it ebbs and it flows, but it is always there. When teachers and students take a stance to harness motivation and use it in productive ways, they meet their goals. Third, this metaphor is powerful because it recognizes that motivation defines the complex relationships among the students, the teacher, and the curriculum.

This metaphor also depicts motivation as an ongoing force or energy that can be tapped into with a result of action, or in the case of classrooms, with a result of engagement. Although often used interchangeably, **motivation** is the energy that can lead to activity or **engagement**. They are related but separate. Thus, none of these factors alone guarantees motivation, but the combination of *particular student qualities* within *facilitative classrooms* working on *certain activities* may effectively harness motivation and result in high levels of engagement.

In this book, we provide teachers with tools that can serve as examples to help them tap into the motivation that is ever-present in the classroom. A variety of motivation manuals are readily available that describe a range of motivation theories or provide lists of simple strategies to motivate students and externally manipulate the environment. While many of these are useful and beneficial in the short term, the tools in this book are not as simple. They are not a "how-to" manual or a recipe that will magically transform a frustrating classroom situation into your version of a teacher's paradise. However, with an understanding of student motivation, plus reflection and effort, teachers may use these tools and others like them to cultivate a classroom environment and create a learning community in which students and the teacher are highly motivated to engage in activity that shapes meaningful learning. Rather than continually "filling up tanks" or "tending gardens," guiding student learning by tapping into motivation becomes a continual journey in which the teacher's expertise at "navigating currents" grows and evolves.

Book Overview

The book is organized into three sections. In Section I, we explore the concept of motivation and address the following questions:

1. What does motivation look like in our students and classrooms?

2. How can teachers assess the nature of motivation in their classroom?

Section I ends with a set of guiding questions for teachers to consider in creating a classroom environment that effectively harnesses motivation in support of student learning. Four questions provide a framework for reflection that we encourage teachers to use when they are interested in enhancing a motivational classroom climate and designing activity that aids their reflective process. However, we invite teachers to engage with these questions in an ongoing, reflective manner with the assumptions that all students can learn and that teaching is a continually evolving craft. The guiding questions we will explore are:

1. How do you provide the opportunity for students to make decisions and express their *voice* in the classroom?

2. What opportunities do you provide for students to engage in *meaningful* and *relevant* work in your classroom?

3. How are students being *challenged* at an appropriate level and supported in being *successful* with those challenges?

4. What are you doing to foster a sense of belonging through peer and student-teacher *relationships* in your classroom?

Section II of the book is divided into four chapters. Each of these chapters is framed by one of these four questions. Each chapter provides a deeper discussion of an essential element of classroom motivation and describes a variety of practices and strategies teachers can use to harness the specific qualities of motivation described in the chapter.

Section III discusses challenges to creating and sustaining high levels of motivation in classrooms and schools. Therefore, the chapters in this section first consider some of obstacles to creating a classroom culture of motivation and then suggest ways to sustain that culture over time. Three questions that help frame this section are:

1. How can you develop and sustain a motivational climate over time?

2. How can you buffer your students from demotivating influences outside your classroom?

3. How can you sustain your own motivation for learning as a way to maintain student motivation?

We hope this book informs teachers' understanding of motivation and encourages them to look beyond simplistic answers to discover how to enhance motivation in the classroom in more depth. In addition to exploring individual and classroom motivational qualities, we use the idea of motivation as always present, like a river current, to illustrate how the motivational qualities of a person are inseparable from their environment. We believe that teachers are guides, navigating learners by working with the current of motivation and adapting their ever-shifting classroom to take full advantage of the collective contributions of all students.

As teachers and teacher educators, we have come to understand the value of self-reflection as a critical tool for improving teaching practice. However, we also acknowledge the complexity of the teaching and learning process for teachers and students. Throughout the book, we provide suggestions for how teachers can employ research-based motivational strategies by taking an open, reflective stance toward their teaching. Moreover, we explore how our actions as teachers are situated within our schools and communities of practice, evolving over time. We focus on understanding shared participation in activity that creates a classroom culture as the place that supports and enhances motivation for achievement rather than depicting classrooms as a place where students arrive with predetermined motivation or as a place where student will be magically transformed by the teacher or curriculum. Our hope is that this focus on shared participation in the activities of teaching and learning captures the complexity of the interactions and work in which teachers and students engage in their classroom.

CHAPTER WRAP-UP ACTIVITY

Use the Frayer Model (see Buehl, 2001) to construct a concept map or graphic organizer of your understanding of "motivation" as it stands after reading the introduction. Each quadrant requires you to elaborate on your definition of motivation by defining, listing characteristics, and considering examples and nonexamples. As you progress through the book, we suggest you return to this model to revise and reconsider your developing understanding of motivation.

(Continued)

(Continued)

Frayer Model	
DEFINITION	**CHARACTERISTICS**
EXAMPLES/MODELS	**NONEXAMPLES**

1

What Is Motivation to Learn?

As we begin our discussion of motivation, we encourage readers to consider their prior experiences and knowledge about motivation. To do this, we ask readers to think of examples of motivated and unmotivated behaviors and the teachers and classrooms that support those behaviors. Each of us can think of students who we might have considered motivated, and we may be able to identify times in our class when we believed we had really created a motivating environment.

ACTIVITY 1.1 REFLECTIVE PRACTICE

Use a class list to identify which students you would consider motivated or unmotivated.

1. What guided your decisions?

2. What did students do to convey motivation or lack of motivation?

3. Why do you think students are or are not motivated?

4. What do you know about their motivation in other classrooms? Is it similar or different from their motivation in your class?

5. How are you defining *motivation?*

SAVE THIS CLASS LIST FOR AN ACTIVITY AT THE END OF THE CHAPTER.

The following scenario depicts several students across classrooms and may provide additional insight into our question of "What is motivation to learn?"

CASE STUDY: RIVER VIEW MIDDLE SCHOOL

As the end of the first marking period was coming to a close, Mr. Martinez watched his Language Arts students as they worked in small groups preparing to write character sketches from the book they just completed and reflected on during the first few weeks of school. The group with Kiko, Rashad, and Jennifer caught his attention.

"Let's make sure we have all of our information organized and make a chart with all the requirements and our responses," barked Jennifer as she typically took charge.

"OK. That's a good idea," responded Rashad, as he had the book open and was rereading it. He was a voracious reader, always with a book in hand even if he had read it two or three times in the past. "I came up with a couple of ideas, but let me look at this section again."

"Come on, Kiko," Jennifer said as she turned her attention to the third member of the group. "You haven't been paying any attention." Kiko continued to talk with her friend at the next table about their soccer game over the weekend.

Since his school required Mr. Martinez to provide a grade for effort on report cards, he wondered how he could capture his students' engagement in any meaningful way through a grade.

He approached the group. "How's your work coming along? Do you have any questions or need any help?"

"Mr. Martinez, we're almost finished with the first part of the assignment," Jennifer offered. "I created a chart to organize us. Rashad is looking for a few more details. But Kiko hasn't been a help at all." Rashad looked up from his book to see what would happen.

"Kiko?" Mr. Martinez asked. "What've you been doing? Have you done any work?"

"Sure, Mr. Martinez," she replied as she swiveled back to the group and produced a half-crumpled sheet of paper with the basic facts needed for the assignment.

The bell rang and students moved along to their next class— math. Ms. O'Brien watched the students file in. She like this particular group but their performance ranged widely, which presented a challenge as she tried to move the class along in the curriculum. This is the last year in which the students will be in a mixed-level math class. At the end of the year, she'd have to recommend which students moved on to Algebra I.

"Please take out your homework so we can begin," she said with a chipper tone. The class responded slowly and most placed their homework on the desk.

A classroom aide nudged Rashad, "Do you have your work today?"

Rashad replied sheepishly, "Um . . . yeah . . . somewhere." He produced a piece of paper with only a few answers on it. It looked

(Continued)

(Continued)

like something he had done quickly during study hall just to get it done. The aide recalled a team meeting with Rashad's parents earlier in the year in which they explained his history with math. "Ever since second grade, he has struggled with math," she remembered Rashad's mother reporting. "At home he can do the math problems if I sit with him, but he freezes up when he works on them alone. Mostly he just tries to avoid math all together."

"Kiko, how did your soccer game go yesterday?" Ms. O'Brien asked as she moved around the class. She enjoyed getting to know her students and following up on their afterschool activities. "Did you also have some time for math last night?"

"Sure did, Ms. O.," Kiko replied. She showed the teacher her homework. "I think I got most of them right. There were a few tricky ones. But you should've seen the goal I almost scored in our game."

"That's great, Kiko."

"Ms. O'Brien," Jennifer called with her hand up. "Are we going to go over the homework as a class? I tried the extra credit problems and could put one of them up on the board."

"Thanks, Jennifer. I might need you to do that."

ACTIVITY 1.2a CASE STUDY ANALYSIS QUESTIONS

Using the River View Middle School example, compare Kiko, Rashad, and Jennifer:

1. How would you describe each student's motivation?

2. What are the behaviors or characteristics that informed you about their motivation?

3. Which student or students would you want in your classroom? Why?

We began our comments on the nature of motivation with a description of three students as they transition through part of their school day. Their motivation can be considered from three perspectives: the individual, the classroom, and the activity of the individual in the context. All three perspectives have theoretical and empirical support, as the following sections illustrate.

Motivation as an Individual Quality

What were the characteristics of the students you viewed as motivated in the scenario or of students you have had in your classroom?

Often, motivation is considered a quality of individuals, such as hair or eye color. In reading this account, it may seem easy to quickly identify the student or students who are motivated to learn in each classroom. In English/Language Arts (ELA), Jennifer appeared very motivated. She participated enthusiastically, dictated the pace of the work for her group, and was eager to assist her teacher. Rashad seemed to have a moderate amount of motivation. His strong interest was in one aspect of the class—reading. Kiko seemed very unmotivated and only gave minimal effort in the class. In Math, Jennifer was again quite motivated and ready to participate fully in the classroom. However, Rashad fell apart when it came to math and avoided his math work. Kiko was uninvolved in English but seemed motivated for math class and eager to relate to her teacher.

However, it is important to remember that the outward behaviors being observed are markers of engagement, not motivation. Motivation is the deeper energy that exists in each learner and has a direction or goal, even if that goal is not aligned with the current classroom goal or is not apparent to the teacher.

When examining motivation as an individual quality, it is often related to a host of individual beliefs and behaviors that signal motivation.

A positive sense of self-efficacy. One individual quality that has been positively related to motivation is a sense of self-efficacy or the belief that you can succeed at a task. Psychologist Albert Bandura (1986) was one of the first to suggest that people are proactive in engaging with the environment as a result of their self-beliefs. He further suggested that a learner's beliefs about their capability are often a better indicator of motivation and success than actual capability. Bandura's suggestions have been supported by several decades of research across age, settings, and subject areas. Students who appear more motivated often have a stronger belief in their ability to succeed than other students. As teachers, we often encounter situations in which a student has given up on the task, exclaiming, "I can't do it!" This student's belief in a lack of ability is influencing his or her motivation and subsequent engagement in the activity.

More recent examinations of self-efficacy have revealed the strength of societal beliefs about people as a result of some identifying characteristic such as race or gender. Steele (1997) and Aronson and Steele (2005) have demonstrated a "stereotype threat" in which a learner underperforms in an activity when stereotypes of that person's race or gender suggest a lack of ability or success and are made salient. In an initial study of this phenomenon, Steele and Aronson (1995) had black and white college students take a GRE test. The black students performed less well on the test. However, when the directions were changed to indicate that the test was not a measurement of intellectual performance, the achievement gap between the two groups was reduced.

Self-efficacy may be based in a student's prior performance or by other factors that lead them to make judgments about their capabilities, leading to a powerful effect on their engagement and on the direction or goal of their motivation.

ACTIVITY 1.2b CASE STUDY ANALYSIS QUESTIONS

1. How would you judge the self-efficacy of each student in the case study and how did their self-efficacy relate to motivation?

2. On what information did you base your conclusions?

3. What actions would you take to enhance self-efficacy for each student?

The belief that success follows proper effort. Beyond believing that you can be successful in a learning activity, another quality of individual motivation is the belief that success comes from proper effort. Most learning activities lead to some judgment of success or failure in the activity. How the learner makes sense of success or failure may indicate the subsequent motivation for that activity. Weiner (1986) describes the role of attributions for success or failure as being related to whether that success or failure is caused by elements within the learner's control, such as effort or persistence, or out of the learner's control, such as bad luck or an overly harsh teacher. For example, two students who take a math test and fail may have very different thoughts. One student may think, "If only I tried harder, I know I could have passed that test." On the other hand, the second student concludes, "My math teacher always gives impossible tests that can't be passed." The student who makes the attribution to effort is more likely to be motivated toward learning in the future.

Carol Dweck (2006) labels this phenomenon as an entity versus incremental approach to intelligence. If you believe your success in any activity, including school, work, or relationships, is because of the effort you expend and that the situation can change over time, you will be more motivated toward continuing that activity. However, if you believe that some fixed quality, such as a lack of ability, leads to failure, you are less likely to be motivated for that activity. In our case study, this seems to be the situation for Rashad who has identified himself as incapable in math. He is less likely to put effort into work he sees as fruitless and more likely to be motivated toward avoiding his math work.

Interest that is enduring rather than situational. Being motivated to engage in an activity is often related to having an interest in that activity. It makes sense that a student who is interested in writing will more happily engage in writing projects in the classroom than in activities that are less interesting to him. Being interested in schoolwork has been shown to be related to a student's attention (Hidi, Renninger & Krapp, 2004) and to higher levels of learning (Alexander, 1997; Renninger

& Hidi, 2002). Researchers Hidi and Renninger (2006) suggest a four-phase model of how interest may develop in a learner. The learner may experience some trigger or hook that generates interest in the moment. Such a situational interest (Phase 1) may be sustained through additional stimulation causing interest to continue (Phase 2). Some situational interests may emerge as initial individual interest (Phase 3) with the goal of forming well-developed individual interest in the activity (Phase 4). For example, a teacher may teach a history lesson on colonial America by having students reenact a typical colonial homestead with costumes, cooking over a fire, and creating tools, clothing, and toys. A student who previously had no interest in history may engage in this activity because it is hands-on and fun. This situational interest may persist over the entire week of the activity. The teacher then may notice the student reading more about colonial America, with the hope that this may lead to a more enduring personal interest in American History. Having students develop an enduring individual interest in their subject area or in schooling itself may be the hope that some teachers hold. When interest progresses to an enduring personal characteristic or well-developed interest, beyond the immediate situation or activity due to its novelty or catchy quality, the learner is more likely to be motivated to continue pursuing this subject area.

Goals for exploration and developing competence. The term "motivation" connotes that a learner is engaging in action toward a particular target. There may be a range of goals related to motivation, including the goal of improving at a task, showing how well you can do something, or social acceptance. In classrooms, the goal of developing or improving competence is known as a mastery goal (Pintrich, 2000) and has been associated with many beneficial educational beliefs and behaviors such as self-efficacy, self-regulation, and positive affect toward school (Kaplan, Middleton, Urdan, & Midgley, 2002). It is often contrasted with a performance goal, or engaging in work for the purpose of demonstrating competence, which has been associated with a range of negative and positive outcomes in the classroom. For example, in a physical education class, a teacher observed a girl shooting the basketball over and over again. She approached the teacher and asked for pointers for playing. Without regard to looking good or making errors, she began incorporating suggestions, working with the teacher and peers, and showed improvement. A student with the goal of getting better in a particular task or subject area will often seek help and view errors as an opportunity to learn. We believe that an important quality of motivation is to possess a mastery goal for learning rather than a performance goal.

Value for the activity and its usefulness. Many students who appear motivated hold value for a task, subject area, or schooling. Value for a learning task may be an inherent value in the activity or may be a perception that the activity has some value or use in the future. This utility value (Wigfield & Eccles, 2000) may change over time depending on the information a student receives or the emphasis placed on a task or subject area by parents, teachers, or other community members. For example, many mathematics teachers seem concerned that their students show low motivation for math. However, students may be renewed in that motivation when they see how math can be used in their daily lives; in other subject areas, such as chemistry and physics; or as a pathway into college or a career. An understanding that content knowledge can be applied or used in the future may be related to a student's motivation. The application or future use of knowledge also plays a role in placing value on a certain activity, subject area, or even school itself. In fact, some students may feel alienated from schooling itself but see school as valuable for its long-term benefit and, therefore, be more motivated toward school.

Display a sense of connection with others. Teachers often notice an engaged student by the way she interacts with the teacher, with other students, and within a learning community. Although intrinsic motivation for an activity, as noted earlier, is an important quality of motivation, activities themselves typically takes place with other people in a particular setting.

Research has shown that students who are motivated in school have strong relationships with teachers and want to develop social relationships with peers (Patrick, Ryan, & Kaplan, 2007; Wentzel, Battle, Russell, & Looney, 2010). These students often have a more positive affect for school and may cope with problems more effectively (Zimmer-Gembeck & Locke, 2007). This social motivation to connect may be especially true for at-risk or traditionally "unmotivated" students for whom social connections are a driving force to attend school. As our vignette of the students at River View Middle School indicates, Jennifer and Kiko appear motivated to engage with the teacher in conversation about social or academic topics. Their work in small groups was facilitated by Jennifer who appeared motivated and eager to engage the other students and the teacher in discussions of their work. As we see with Kiko, even talk that may be considered nonacademic, off task, or social may be interrelated with the work of school and may act as an entry point for some students who seem reluctant. In general, the students who have a sense of belonging seem happier and connected to school.

Summary. Defining motivation in terms of these individual qualities and behaviors aligns with the metaphor of motivation as a gas tank. The "motivational tank" is seen as full, empty, or somewhere in between based on outward behaviors. This is a very common way for teachers to discuss and think about motivation. This view can be examined by considering each of the students in our case study, as we did at the start of this section. Kiko, Rashad, and Jennifer all may be described by their level of motivation. Each portrays a level of interest, confidence, value, and connection to their classroom work. As teachers, it is tempting to think about our students as they appear in front of us and imbue them with certain fixed qualities regarding their motivation.

Motivation as a Classroom Quality

Although students may seem to arrive in our classrooms as motivated or unmotivated, many experiences in their lives may have contributed to those qualities we have described.

ACTIVITY 1.3 REFLECTIVE PRACTICE

Which of the following are the three most common reasons for the motivated beliefs and behaviors of your students?

- Positive experience with an activity or subject
- Parents' interests and beliefs
- Parental expectations for grades or performance
- Peers' value for learning
- Teacher support
- Observing someone engaged in an activity
- Social and economic opportunity
- Beliefs or stereotypes about an activity
- Self-identity
- Past experience with a teacher or in school

One factor that seems intimately linked to a student's motivation is experience and participation in the classroom. In the Introduction, the metaphor that aligned with the classroom being the primary factor in motivation is that of gardening. In this metaphor, the quality of soil, light, and moisture may contribute to a plant's growth. In the classroom, this suggests that the curriculum, activities, and qualities of the teacher and instruction would be the source of motivation. Although some teachers may believe that there is little they can do in the classroom to impact motivation, anecdotal evidence and research both suggest that teachers and classrooms do matter. In fact, the instructional and psychological environments of classrooms have been consistently related to the motivation reported by individual students (Meece, Anderman & Anderman, 2006).

In our example of River View Middle School, Rashad, Kiko, and Jennifer were motivated differently in different classrooms. You may recall from your education that some classes were more motivating than others for you. Those classrooms may have differed by subject area and grade level. Nevertheless, each classroom has its own motivational culture or climate. As frequent observers of classrooms, we have often noticed and discussed how some classrooms seem to have a motivational energy or quality that students perceive and act on.

ACTIVITY 1.4 CASE STUDY ANALYSIS QUESTIONS

1. How does each student's motivation shift across classrooms in the case study? Why?

2. What qualities of the classroom seem to influence the students' motivation?

3. How would each of these students react to your classroom?

In fact, the investigation of how classroom characteristics relate to student beliefs and behaviors has a long history (e.g., Moos, 1979; Walberg & Anderson, 1968). Researchers using achievement goal theory have examined not only students' individual motivation but also their perceptions of the goals that are emphasized in their classroom. Therefore, students may hold their personal goals for learning and they may also perceive the goals emphasized in the classroom. For example, when students perceive their classrooms as emphasizing improving their competence, then they are more likely to hold those same personal goals.

A classroom's motivational climate is important for at least two reasons. First, the classroom climate provides the setting for a student's experience. Their perceptions of themselves, their academic work, and their social interactions are filtered through how they experience the classroom climate. Second, classroom climate may act as a buffer to other contextual influences. For example, even in an overall climate of high-stakes testing, a classroom climate that emphasizes student autonomy and community building may lead to more beneficial motivational patterns in students (Ciani, Middleton, Summers, & Sheldon, 2010). Next we consider the motivational qualities of the classroom environment through three areas: instructional practices, curriculum, and teacher characteristics.

Instructional Practices

Instructional practices are multifaceted in their influence on student motivation. Instructional practice determines the activities in which students and teachers participate as they try to meet the objectives or standards of the class. At the same time, instruction can take place in a variety of formats—whole group instruction, small group instruction, or individual instruction. Teachers can also develop very different general approaches to their instruction. Some believe in strong teacher-centered instruction, in which information is conveyed to students, often in lecture format. At the other end of the continuum, a teacher may serve more as a facilitator by questioning the learner to construct understanding. Instructional practice also encompasses the rules and regulations that guide classroom behavior—from a strict rewards-based management system to allowing students to make and enforce their own rules.

Teachers often discuss and consider the instructional practices that might work best in their classroom. Those discussions are sometimes based on personal experience in the classroom and sometimes based on educational research. The United States Department of Education developed a "What Works" clearinghouse for research on instruction as a way to help educators make informed choices on instructional approaches (www.ies.ed.gov/ncee/wwwc/). Rather than providing generalized information, the website allows educators to examine research-based information on the content area (literacy, mathematics, or science), outcomes (achievement, dropout prevention, and student behavior) and student characteristics (early childhood, youth with disabilities, adolescents, and English Language Learners) to determine what practices may be most effective. Recently, some researchers (e.g., Marzano, 2003; Hattie, 2009; 2012; Marzano, 2003) have also employed metaanalysis research to identify factors and variables that have been shown to have the greatest impact on student achievement.

As discussed in Section II of this book, teachers are in a position of making many daily choices about instructional strategies or approaches. We advocate for those decisions to be made with an open stance toward new ideas, with a solid understanding of educational research, with the use of data-driven decision making, and with attention to how the range of instructional practices in which a teacher engages are consistent or aligned toward the same goal.

No matter what your instructional approach is in your classroom, you are sending messages to students about your expectations for their engagement and motivation. At times, those messages may be conflicting. For example, a teacher may want to emphasize mastery goals in the classroom by choosing open-ended, highly engaging tasks but may diminish the motivational impact of those activities by choosing assessments that compare students and provide only one opportunity for success—thus emphasizing performance goals.

ACTIVITY 1.5 CRITICAL REFLECTION

1. How would your students characterize your instructional practices?

2. How do you think your instructional choices relate to student motivation in your classroom?

Catch and hold. Using the notion of situational interest, Mitchell (1993) describes an instruction process of "catch and hold" to build student interest in the classroom. This process involves "catching" interest through novel, fun, or intriguing episodes such as group work, technology, and games; then, the teacher works to "hold" interest by showing the value and meaningfulness of work or by enhancing student involvement.

One instructional approach some teachers believe will provide the initial catch to motivate students is to view teaching as a performance and adopt an energetic, theatrical manner in the classroom—for example, a teacher who conveys enthusiasm through tone, gestures, and action. Sarason (1999) likens teaching to a performing art in his specific call for teacher training programs to encourage new teachers to consider how content is presented in the classroom. This notion of teaching as artistry may resonate with those who recall teachers whose charismatic presence drew them into the classroom.

Thinking about instruction as a performance may help students attend during a particular moment in class. However, attention or an episodic alertness tied to a teacher's instructional style may not hold or result in sustained engagement in the activity or content of learning. We make the strong distinction between ways to catch interest that may result in short-term attention and those that tap into motivation that is enduring or can hold a student.

A similar phenomenon is presenting a question, media clip, contradiction, phenomenon, or object as a hook to begin a lesson. In *Teach Like a Champion*, Lemov (2010) suggests that successful teachers grab immediate attention in the classroom by presenting a hook. That hook draws students into class by eliminating outside distractions or competing demands. The hook can serve as an introduction to the content and may be a reference point throughout the lesson.

The performance and hook approaches to motivating students may provide an initial sense of engagement in the classroom and certainly can be useful as an initial management strategy to start a class. However, all of us who have taught know that our students are subject to the "attention curve" or the tendency to pay attention to the beginning and end of a presentation with a large drop-off in attention in the middle. If a motivational approach involves a performance, hooks, or props, teaching may become an endless cycle of novelty with little-sustained work or focus. The follow-up hold through deep involvement or meaningfulness of work (Mitchell, 1993) is essential.

Learning styles. Although not supported by research, but often discussed among practitioners, another instructional approach that has received attention for improving student engagement is to consider students' learning styles when planning instruction. The learning styles movement suggests that matching instruction to the biological and emotional preferences of students will result in engagement and learning. One example of this movement is Kolb's (1984) learning style inventory that is often used to determine the patterns of behavior students exhibit based on experience and background. In this theory, learning emerges along two dimensions (concrete-abstract and doing-watching) to form four patterns of learning (see Table 1.1).

Since learners may exhibit different patterns of learning, Kolb (1984) suggests that the best learning environment to engage students depends on balancing these modes of thinking. For example, a student with an accommodating learning style might be more motivated to learn about force and motion by crashing cars with different weights into an increasing number of weighted blocks and measuring the impact. That trial and error might align to the students' preferred way of learning and reinforce the academic content.

Despite the prevalence of discussion regarding implementation of learning styles in classrooms, there is reason for caution. McKeachie (1995) warns educators that "styles are often taken to be fixed, inherited characteristics that limit students' ability to learn in ways that do not fit their styles" (p. 1) and

Table 1.1   Kolb's Styles of Learning

	Reflective	Active
Concrete	**Diverging** (concrete, reflective)—emphasizes the innovative and imaginative approach to doing things	**Accommodating** (concrete, active)—uses trial and error rather than thought and reflection.
Abstract	**Assimilating** (abstract, reflective)—pulls a number of different observations and thoughts into an integrated whole	**Converging** (abstract, active)—emphasizes the practical application of ideas and solving problems

that the only way for students to learn is by matching learning style to instruction. The reliance on such a match could ultimately lead to diminishing motivation and engagement for a broad range of activities and in many subject areas for students. Instead, McKeachie suggests that teachers help students develop skills and strategies to become more effective learners and motivate them for continued learning. In the case of student learning about force and motion through trial tests in physics, that student may also be engaged in the prediction-observation-reflection cycle of learning science to develop skills of abstract thinking, and he may be asked to develop new tests of force and motion to learn to apply ideas.

Classrooms that value multiple intelligences. Gardner's (1999) theory of multiple intelligences provides a different kind of roadmap for adapting instruction to meet students' strengths, abilities, and interests and to develop areas that may be less strong. Multiple intelligence theory suggests that there is a broad range of cognitive abilities that are not strongly correlated, including the following:

- Logical-mathematical: conceptual and abstract thinking about numerical and logical patterns
- Spatial: ability to visualize abstractly and think in graphics and pictures
- Linguistic: verbal skills; understanding the sounds and meaning of words
- Bodily-kinesthetic: skillfully control the body and manipulate objects
- Musical: capacity to understand rhythm, sound pattern, and pitch
- Interpersonal: interpret and respond appropriately to others' thoughts and internal states
- Intrapersonal: self-awareness and insight into own thoughts, feelings, and values
- Naturalistic: sense of place in nature; including recognizing objects, plants, and animals
- Existential: capability of addressing questions of deep meaning related to human existence

In *Multiple Intelligences in the Classroom,* Armstrong (2009) provides ways for teachers to assess students' intelligences and provides examples of classroom activities that access and promote each intelligence. In working with teachers across many different settings, we have found that teachers often make a conscious effort of providing a variety of ways for students to access and demonstrate knowledge in line with Gardner's theory. By taking a multiple intelligences approach in the classroom, a teacher may be tapping into the motivational current by increasing student sense of self-efficacy and by providing comfortable opportunities for initial engagement with content.

TARGET. A widely known way to understand classroom instructional practices that relate to motivation is through the acronym TARGET. Based on the work of Epstein (1989) and Ames (1992) the motivational quality of classrooms may be thought of according to the acronym TARGET, which stands for the following.

Task: the manner in which teachers structure tasks and learning activities

Autonomy: the locus of responsibility in the classroom

Recognition: the appearance, purpose, and types of recognition used in the classroom

Grouping: how students are arranged to work together

Evaluation: the informal and formal ways students are assessed and evaluated

Time: how time is used to manage classroom activities

This approach to examining classroom motivation was modified into a classroom observation system in the *Observing Patterns of Adaptive Learning* manual (OPAL; Patrick, et al., 1997; Patrick, Anderman, Ryan, Edelin, & Midgley, 2001) to assess the motivational climate of a classroom, expanding on the original TARGET categories by adding "social" features of the classroom. In exploring the nature of classroom motivation with a group of teachers, Midgley and her colleagues, developed a list of practices (See Table 1.2) for moving from a performance-focused classroom to a mastery-focused classroom. The full report to teachers can be found at http://www.umich.edu/~pals/pals/hs_feedback_report.PDF.

Table 1.2   Strategies to Move Toward a Mastery-Focused Middle School Environment

	Move Away From	**Move Toward**
Grouping	Grouping by ability	Grouping by topic, interest, student choice; frequent reformation of groups
Competition/ Cooperation	Competition between students; contests with limited winners	Cooperative learning
Assessment	Using test data as a basis for comparison; over-use of standardized tests	Using test data for diagnosis; alternatives to tests such as portfolios
Grading	Normative grading; public display of grades	Grading for progress, improvement; involving students in determining their grades
Recognition/ Rewards/ Incentives	Recognition for relative performance; honor rolls for high grades; over-use of praise, especially for the completion of short, easy tasks	Recognition of progress, improvement; an emphasis on learning for its own sake
Student Input	Decisions made exclusively by administrators and teachers	Opportunities for choice, electives; student decision making, self-scheduling, self-regulation

(Continued)

Table 1.2   (Continued)

	Move Away From	Move Toward
Approaches to the Curriculum	Departmentalized approach to curriculum	Thematic approaches/ interdisciplinary focus; viewing mistakes as part of learning; allowing students to redo work; encouraging students to take academic risks
Academic Tasks	Rote learning and memorization; over-use of worksheets and textbooks; decontextualizing facts	Providing challenging, complex work to students; giving homework that is enriching and challenging; encouraging problem solving and comprehension
Remediation	Pull-out programs; retention	Cross-age tutoring; peer tutoring; enrichment
These strategies serve as examples. Strategies will depend on the characteristics of the school, the identified needs, and the preferences of the school staff. Strategies such as cross-age grouping, block scheduling, small house, and team teaching, although not listed here, are recommended as enabling mechanisms.		

It is important to note the pressure teachers may experience because of an emphasis on standardized testing in their school or community. Even when teachers are knowledgeable about best practices, those practices may be difficult to implement due to time constraints, standardization of curriculum, or other pressures. The notion of classrooms as part of a larger system of schooling, including the pressures that come from outside the classroom, is explored more fully in Section 3.

Curriculum

Curriculum defines the objectives, content, and activities in which a teacher engages students. From the standpoint of our metaphor for motivation, the curriculum is the river in which the motivational current exists and, therefore, shapes the potential of motivation. The curriculum stands apart from daily instructional choices about tasks, choice, and grouping that are described earlier and define the larger structure of what happens in the classroom. Some curricula are developed by curriculum experts for teachers to implement (e.g., *Everyday Math*); whereas, other curricula are based on a set of design principles (e.g., Expeditionary Learning or project-based science) or are developed locally by a teacher or team of teachers. Increasingly, we see curricula tied to local, state, or national standards for grade levels and content areas (e.g., Common Core State Standards, Next Generation Science Standards, etc.).

The curriculum chosen or developed for a classroom may be considered as more or less motivating for students. Teachers may use its motivational properties as one of the evaluation criteria in choosing a curriculum to use in the classroom. In our work with teachers, in our own classrooms, and in research, several qualities of curricula emerge as influencing its motivational strength.

Inquiry-Based Curricula

These types of curricula emphasize student exploration of broad ideas by gathering, evaluating, and presenting data. Students are able to draw conclusions about content through their own systematic exploration or a guiding question. Often inquiry-based projects are focused on guiding questions that are interesting or relevant to students' lives, involve collaboration with other students, and require presentation of results. These curricula may relate to engagement through the open-ended nature of tasks, potential to work with students, and the accountability of presenting findings.

Applied Curricula

Applied curricula engage students by relating content to real-world problems or everyday life. Students consider the way academic content is used on a daily basis or to answer questions that may improve our communities, families, or lives. By incorporating content that is relevant/applicable to their lives and/or communities, the value of the academic task is increased. Motivation theory suggests that enhanced value will also relate to enhanced motivation.

Thematic Curricula

Thematic curricula focus on content that may have particular appeal to students based on interest or novelty and are often centered on a guiding question. Students pursue a topic deeply during a thematic curriculum to master content or draw broader conclusions across content areas. Similarly to applied curriculum, thematic curricula activate motivation by increasing task value. This type of curriculum also has the potential to provide choice for students on what they study or how they engage in academic work.

ACTIVITY 1.6 APPLICATION TO PRACTICE

Think of examples of curricula that fall into the categories described earlier. They may be a standard curriculum that you or your school adopted or may be curricula that you or your colleagues created for your classroom. What aspects of your examples leverage motivation in your students?

Curriculum Type	Examples	Motivators?
Inquiry-based		
Applied		

Curriculum Type	Examples	Motivators?
Thematic		
Other		

Teacher Qualities

Another set of characteristics of classrooms that relate to motivation are the personal qualities of the teachers that go beyond their instructional approach or the curriculum being used. Often, we hear students remark that they are motivated to attend or participate in a class because of the teacher. Indeed, the relationship between a student and teacher often makes a difference in students' classroom experiences and, in particular, can engage otherwise reluctant students. Teachers who exhibit qualities such as warmth, reliability, fairness, respect, and humor or who have enthusiasm or interest in the subject area are often seen as motivating. In her book *Teacher Leadership that Strengthens Professional Practice* (2006), Charlotte Danielson names a number of dispositions or traits with which teachers approach situations that are related to effective teaching. A professional demeanor that builds a teachers' standing as a teacher leader and as a motivating teacher might include the following:

- A deep commitment to student learning
- Optimism and enthusiasm
- Open-mindedness and humility
- Courage to take risks
- Confidence
- Tolerance for ambiguity
- Perseverance

A strong component of students' motivational history is the support they have experienced by parents and teachers and the emotions associated with learning (McCaslin, 2009; McClelland, 1985). McCaslin (2009) describes the process of coregulation of motivation in which students engage in classroom activities but also learn about themselves through the way teachers shape those opportunities and respond to student actions. For example, teachers' dispositions directly contribute to the sense of the classroom as a safe place to work, make mistakes, and take risks, which are important elements of motivated behavior. A classroom in which students feel a sense of belonging, personal support, and support for learning provides the opportunity for a focus on motivation for learning rather than focusing on conflicting motivations. Meeting the psychological needs of students through creating predictable, positive, and emotionally and personally supportive environments provides an "area of comfort" (Simmons & Blythe, 1987) or a stage-environment fit (e.g., Eccles & Midgley, 1989) that is the basis for meaningful engagement.

Teacher caring and commitment. Students respond to the personal qualities of caring and commitment that teachers exhibit toward them. Wilson and Corbett (2001) in *Listening to Urban Kids* report the results of interviews of urban middle school students. Those students described the teachers who were most inspiring and motivating as those who displayed a certain type of care. To those students, caring teachers were the teachers who "stay on them" and don't let them get away with easy work. These teachers provided extra help, held high expectations, and maintained an orderly, organized learning environment. Our research further supports the notion that teachers who are both demanding and supportive, or press students rather than pressuring them (Middleton & Midgley, 2002; Middleton, 2004) are motivating for students.

Teacher passion and interest. An important and often overlooked quality of teachers in motivating students is their passion or interest in learning a particular subject matter. Thompson & Mazer (2012) found that students are more energized and engaged toward a subject when their teacher exhibits verbal and nonverbal communication behaviors such as eye contact, facial expressions, and vocal emphasis as well as clearly presenting subject matter. It seems that students are constantly reading cues from their teachers about interest and passion for learning course content and adapt their own interest and engagement when they sense those qualities in their teacher.

ACTIVITY 1.7 CRITICAL REFLECTION

Use the questions and table of Danielson's professional dispositions to reflect on the personal qualities you bring to the classroom that relate to student motivation.

What do you say or do that show Danielson's professional dispositions?

How do these actions influence student motivation in your classroom?

Teacher Quality	Evidence	Motivational Outcome
A deep commitment to student learning		
Optimism and enthusiasm		
Open-mindedness and humility		
Courage to take risks		
Confidence		
Tolerance for ambiguity		
Perseverance		

A New Way to Think About Student Motivation to Learn

Both conceptions of motivation presented so far—an individual quality and a classroom quality—provide insight into what we can observe about motivation in our case study of

River View Middle School. However, by themselves, they do not fully capture the dynamic and complex nature of motivation. Our consideration of the case study and of the metaphor of motivation as a river current lead to two main features of the definition of motivation: its situational nature and its consistency. Therefore, we conclude that motivation to learn appears in activity between students and teacher as they engage in the work of their classroom. None of the individual and classroom factors described early guarantee motivation *by itself*, but it is the combination of *particular student qualities* within *facilitative classrooms* working on *certain tasks* that result in motivated activity.

Motivation to learn is situated in the activity. As easily as we could describe students' height, eye color, or hair color, we can describe the quantity of motivation each possesses. However, a closer examination reveals that motivation is always situated in a particular context of a social group, learning activity, and community practice at a particular moment. From this perspective, motivation has a situational quality such as courage or kindness that may exist within an individual but will only emerge during certain moments as compared to a fixed quality such as one's physical appearance that is always apparent. In both the gas tank and garden metaphors, motivation is dependent on the fixed qualities of the learner (for example, interest, self-efficacy, or persistence) or fixed qualities of the learning environment (for example, inquiry based curriculum, dynamic teacher, or novel activity). Therefore, we must go back to the metaphor of motivation as a current in a river. Motivated actions or ideas, such as acts of kindness, may not be apparent but will emerge in certain situations when there is an immediate object of, or cause for, action. The interaction of a person in a situation at a given moment embodies motivation. Although the current of motivation is ever-present, it requires directional activity to be channeled or leveraged into a productive force.

We can also recognize that even for students who we would consider highly motivated, their behavior is variable within and across classrooms. The student who is eager to participate in a historical simulation in social studies may be easily distracted during a social studies lecture, silent sustained reading time, or in a group lab in science class. We see this variability in our case study of River View Middle School. Jennifer seemed highly motivated across both English and math classrooms. She was an eager participant, followed directions, organized her group, and produced work. Rashad, on the other hand, seemed engaged in English because of his interest in reading; however, in math, his lack of self-efficacy led him to shut down and withdraw from participation. Finally, Kiko was uninterested in English, seemed distracted and provided little energy or support toward the group projects, but in math, her interest was apparent as she was eager to engage her teacher in conversation and completed her homework assignment.

From these descriptions, it would be a challenge to label any of the students as "motivated" or "unmotivated" because their actions vary across situations, and it would be a challenge to label any classroom as "motivating" or "unmotivating" since the student response to each classroom varied. The case study students, our own students, and even our own motivations, reveal the dynamic and situational nature of motivation for a particular activity at a certain time (See Figure 1.1.).

Motivation to learn is always present. Although educators frame motivation to learn as focused on academic work, all of us experience motivation for different outcomes even in a single setting. As mentioned previously, students have competing motivations in the classroom—academic work, social relationships, or maintaining identity—as well as competing motivations outside of school. For example, Kiko completed her math homework in Ms. O'Brien's class, but her social goal of connecting with that teacher may be the more relevant object of her motivation than the academic work. Ms. O'Brien was able to tap into that motivation current as a way to "catch" Kiko and then "hold" her interest in the subject. Rashad was engaged in English class where his interest in the curriculum was the right means for tapping into the current

Figure 1.1   Motivation as the Intersection of Student, Classroom, and Activity

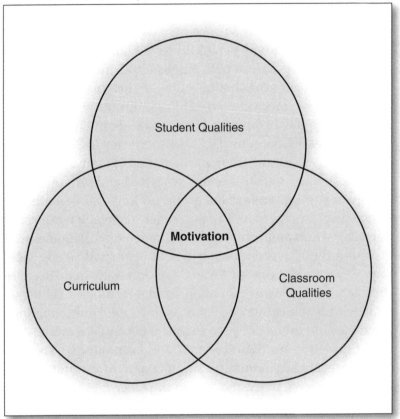

to move along. Finally, Jennifer appeared motivated in both classrooms; however, her motivation may have been focused on "doing school" and being a good student rather than a passion for the academic content. Because the teachers' management and established routines of these classrooms fit into a traditional notion of "doing school," the setting and teaching were a good match for Jennifer's motive and allowed her to engage with the content. These students are motivated, but perhaps not for the academic reasons their teacher would like that motivation to be focused on. If you have tried paddling a canoe in a different direction than the flow of a current, you know the challenge a teacher faces when the direction of a student's motivation is in conflict with academic work. The teachers' work then requires being responsive to the current or energy of students and their motives by shaping an appropriate curriculum with content and instructional practices that "catch" the current and get them moving downstream. Of course, this requires a dynamic approach to navigating the boat through the river while taking into account the disruptions and changes in the current, as well as the external obstacles that impede progress.

Our premise that motivation to learn is the joint activity of students and teachers while engaged in meaningful work rejects the characterization that some students may be "unmotivated" as an explanation for underachievement in school. Instead, we align with motivation theorists who tell us that student motivation is tightly interwoven with school as a social and cultural practice that integrates the beliefs and values of that community (Hickey, 2003). Students are always motivated for something although sometimes they engage in behaviors or hold attitudes that hinder academic performance when those motives conflict with academic motivation. In our research, talking with students from a variety of communities and backgrounds has supported this premise (e.g., Middleton, Dupuis & Tang, 2013; Middleton, Seaman, & Rheingold, 2012; Perks, 2005; Perks & Middleton, 2006). We certainly talked with students who showed great passion for their subject matter. A student in a middle school social studies class studying pioneers of the civil rights movement responded to a question about people who would challenge the notion that he and his classmates were historians by responding that those people "don't know about us and our work then." On the other hand, we have also talked with students who undermined their own academic performance in their local school because of the fear of having to attend a larger, regional secondary school away from home if they were successful. Their ties to family and community drove their seemingly unmotivated behavior.

Students form their identities as learners, including their motivation, based on the social and cultural practices that are closely related to schooling. Motivation for learning a subject is connected to how that content is put into practice, the language and examples used to illustrate that content, and how it relates to students, their families, and their communities.

As we move forward, we ask that you consider motivation not as a quality of an individual or a quality of the teacher/classroom, but as the shared activity of students and teachers as they engage in meaningful work that shapes their identity as learners. To realign our conceptions of motivation as situated in relationships as students engage in work, we often have to consider the beliefs as teachers that may facilitate or hinder moving forward. We will explore the notion of teacher beliefs and student motivation more deeply in Chapter 2.

CHAPTER WRAP-UP ACTIVITY

Return to your class list and evaluate which perspective would support the reasons you listed for students' motivation or lack of motivation to learn.

How might the reasons that focused on individual qualities be related to classroom characteristics?

How might the reasons about classroom characteristics be related to individual qualities that are changeable?

What are the cultural practices of the school and community that may support the notion of certain students as motivated or unmotivated?

2

How Do Teacher Beliefs Influence Student Motivation?

E ducators are always looking for new strategies to improve instruction and student learning. In our work with pre-service and inservice teachers, educators frequently state that they want to learn strategies to increase student motivation. We assume most readers who will read this book also are looking for concrete strategies to improve student motivation and engagement in their classrooms. However, while most of the chapters in this book describe practical techniques, building motivation does not begin with practices or strategies. Despite their importance, strategies are only part of what constitutes effective practice.

Effective practice springs from a foundation of a teacher's essential assumptions and beliefs about teaching and learning because as teachers we tend to act in ways that support our beliefs. In the previous chapter, our goal was to rethink conceptions of motivation to focus on its situated and continuous nature.

In this chapter, we describe *supportive motivational assumptions and beliefs* as principles a teacher must endorse to harness and sustain high levels of motivation. If a teacher does not support these principles, we believe that student motivation to learn will continue to be elusive. Teachers also need to take a *teaching stance* during instruction that prepares them to behave and react to the constant changes in classroom life in ways that support their beliefs about student motivation to learn. Only when teachers act in ways that support beliefs aligned with what we know from motivation research will they be able to implement practices and motivational strategies in the most effective manner.

ASSUMPTIONS ABOUT TEACHING AND LEARNING

Teacher assumptions have a powerful influence on what students experience and how they respond during learning activities (Demanet & Van Houtte, 2004). Because teachers usually act in accordance with their assumptions, students often respond in commensurate ways. For example, if a teacher assumes that every student can and will learn, then the teacher is more likely to design instruction to ensure success for each student and is less likely to accept failure from any student. Since much of our behavior is influenced by our beliefs as well as by what others believe about us, it is important to consider how teacher beliefs influence student motivation for learning.

Next, we describe two assumptions that are essential for capturing motivation in the classroom. We encourage you to consider each assumption thoughtfully and assess your beliefs regarding these statements. One reason for this critical reflection is that the more we are aware of our assumptions, the more likely we will act in accordance with them. For example, many people support the assumption that humans can contribute to the sustainability of our planet; however, many people may not make recycling a regular practice. The more that the underlying assumption is made conscious in daily thinking and discourse, the more likely the supporting behavior will follow.

Examining teacher assumptions is also important for understanding motivation because we may uncover beliefs that contribute to motivational problems in the classroom. Our behaviors as educators have their roots in our assumptions about teaching and learning. By being explicit about our assumptions, we can fundamentally understand and support motivation in the classroom. We also have to be aware of our assumptions to change them or identify behaviors that may contradict them. In this chapter, we hope to challenge assumptions that may hinder student motivation.

By reflecting on and analyzing our assumptions and behaviors as teachers, we can identify what we truly believe and if we are behaving in a way that supports those beliefs. Therefore, we strongly encourage readers to consider each assumption in the next section. As you do this, think about classroom situations where the assumption might have been tested.

ACTIVITY 2.1 CRITICAL REFLECTION

Write a description of a recent classroom situation in which a student or students did not appear to be motivated toward the learning activity and your instructional goals. Then answer the following questions:

1. Why do you believe the students were not motivated?

2. How did you react?

3. How were your actions aligned with or not aligned with your assumptions about student motivation to learn?

4. In what ways was the situation difficult at the time it occurred? What makes the situation difficult to analyze now?

5. What beliefs did your behavior reflect to the students?

6. What would you do differently if a similar situation occurred again?

7. What belief(s) would you be acting on in this do-over?

Assumption 1—All Students Can and Will Learn

This first assumption for fostering a culture of motivation to learn emphasizes that all students *can* learn; this assumption sets up the expectation that all students *will* learn. Why is this important enough to be our leading statement on teaching and learning? It is important because it embraces our primary task as educators. When we become educators, we accept the responsibility to have a positive impact on students. This responsibility obligates us to create conditions for success for each student. We are unable to fulfill our obligation if we believe that some students cannot learn or expect that some will not learn. Consider any sports team that enters an important game. Very few teams will be successful if they enter the game with their coach assuming they cannot win. It is important to enter the contest with someone guiding the team who has confidence in the players' capabilities. For teachers, it is not only important that they enter learning situations with such confidence; it is *essential*.

When teachers approach teaching with the assumption that all students can and will learn, the potential impact is strongly positive. Researchers have known this for a long time. For example, in one study researchers Rosenthal and Jacobson (1968) administered IQ tests to elementary school students. They randomly chose 20% of the students and told their teachers that these students could be expected to outperform their classmates. At the end of the year, all children were given the same IQ test. The average scores increased, but more dramatically for the first and second graders identified as out-performers. The researchers concluded that a so-called Pygmalion Effect was in operation—teacher expectations for success led to success, particularly for younger children. In a more recent and local example, not too long ago one of us was working with a struggling reader in high school. This student had been diagnosed with Fetal Alcohol Syndrome. Many of her advocates criticized the reading teacher and others for putting the student in the reading class. Some explicitly stated that she would never be able to read at a proficient level. These teachers cared deeply about her and strongly believed that the class would be too stressful. Nonetheless, the reading teacher believed that all of her students were capable of learning to read. She emphasized that with hard work and perseverance by both teacher and student, this student could become a proficient reader. In less than two years, this student went from reading at the fourth grade level to the tenth grade level.

The impact of teacher assumptions can be profoundly negative when we believe students will not learn something we are teaching. Consider the common practice of giving students failing grades. What happens when a student receives a failing grade on an assignment, test, or project without having the opportunity to learn from the failure? What happens when this process repeats itself? How does grading and a willingness to let students fail reflect a belief that some students cannot or will not learn no matter what we do? In short, many students believe not only that they did not learn what was expected of them, but also that they cannot learn it based in part on the belief of their teachers. How often have we heard students say, "I'm terrible at math!" or "I am just not a good writer!" Why would students who continually fail be motivated to persevere? This phenomenon known as "learned helplessness" results in students who mistakenly believe they cannot improve performance (Diener & Dweck, 1978).

Conversely, teachers who hold a strong sense of self-efficacy for their teaching expect positive outcomes for their students in the classroom. Teacher efficacy is the belief that effortful teaching will result in student success (Woolfolk & Hoy, 2004) and has been associated with student achievement (Anderson, Green, & Loewen, 1988; Ashton & Webb, 1986; Ross, 1994) and with students' sense of efficacy (Midgley et al., 1989). Moreover, this impact can be stronger when experienced by a group of teachers. "The perceptions of teachers in a school that the efforts of the faculty as a whole will have a positive effect on students" (Goddard, Hoy, & Woolfolk, 2000) is known as collective efficacy and is likely to result in positive student outcomes.

These examples emphasize the importance of holding and communicating the assumption that all students can and will learn. While individual teachers have limited power to alter institutional practices such as issuing grades, we all have the power to communicate to students that we believe that every single one of them can and will learn and buffer the negative effects of grades or high-stakes testing (Ciani, Middleton, Summers, & Sheldon, 2010). We can also make sure that our classroom practices support this message and do not contradict it.

ACTIVITY 2.2 REFLECTION QUESTION

Here is an item that could appear on a teacher efficacy survey. Which response fits for you?

When I make an effort, I can get results from even the most difficult student in my classroom.

Not at all true		Somewhat true		Very true
1	2	3	4	5

How would you rate your assumptions that you can help your students succeed?
What factors weigh in to your belief?
How do you think this belief impacts your students?

Assumption 2—All Students Are Motivated to Learn

The second assumption about motivation and learning acknowledges what we have found to be the euphemistic "elephant in the room." It asserts that all students are not only able to learn but also motivated to learn. We implore all readers of this book to adopt this assumption. Of the two assumptions we suggest, this seems to be the more challenging of the two for some teachers to embrace. Reasons for this are understandable.

Most of us do not have difficulty envisioning or remembering students who sit with arms folded and face scowling during a lesson or activity. For one of us working as a teacher in an alternative school for students who had been unsuccessful in a traditional high school setting, a group of boys in Algebra I comes to mind. Many of these boys had failed the class the year before and entered the new year seemingly with an attitude to have that happen again. After a couple of weeks without success at connecting with them, one day, the lesson was put aside in favor of a discussion: What do you think of math? Many didn't like it based on previous experiences and felt as though they couldn't succeed. Can you think of other classes that interest you? A few different answers emerged, but several replied, "woodshop." After making arrangements with the woodshop teacher, the class began going into the shop every week to work on projects but with the math behind those projects being made explicit. This activity seemed to tap into the students' existing motivation for understanding how math worked in relation to their projects. This example is not meant to encourage every math teacher to start woodworking with their class, but it is meant to provide an example of the power of identifying the motivation that does exist in our students and using that as a starting point for creatively approaching our teaching to leverage that existing motivation.

When faced with similar scenarios, to what do we attribute the lack of motivation? Is it a lack of motivation to learn on the part of the students? Or do we attribute it to our failure to connect what *we* want students to do with what *they* want to do? Another way to think about this is to ask the following question: Were the students not motivated to learn or was their motivation hidden by other motivations—such as social goals, the desire not to appear incompetent, or avoiding schooling (as opposed to learning)—that were taking priority? In other words, were they motivated but just not motivated to do *what we wanted them to do* at that time?

At times, students may feel a disconnect between their motivation and their perception of the motive for schooling.

As a result, their behaviors or affect toward school may give the appearance of low or no motivation; however, we believe that every student is always motivated for something. Their motivation may not be aligned at a particular time with the motivation their teacher would like.

In our years working with teachers and students across many different settings, we have found that students, even the most disengaged students, want to succeed, want to do meaningful, important work, and want to have meaningful social connection in their lives at school. In our classrooms, we have met challenges with a variety of learners, and have not always experienced successful outcomes. However, in taking the time to talk with our students and their families, our belief that every student has motivation to succeed has been always been reaffirmed. One of us received a note from a former student who had not been successful in class. In her note, she apologized for some of her behaviors but wanted to express her appreciation at the effort and belief in her that she experienced in class. At that time, she could not find a way to overcome some of the more immediate challenges she was facing to put effort into the class even though she wanted to. She explained that she later reentered school, graduated, attended community college, and was happily working as a preschool teacher.

An explanation of why it is so important to assume that all students are motivated to learn relates back to our earlier description of Weiner's Attribution Theory (Weiner, 1986). This theory describes the importance of how we think about success and failure. Individuals who attribute success and failure to their efforts tend to operate from an internal locus of control. People who consider outside factors to be responsible for accomplishments and setbacks tend to have an external locus of control. In general, individuals who hold themselves responsible for successes and failures tend to be more motivated than individuals who hold external forces responsible. These individuals also tend to persevere when confronted with obstacles. As teachers, we can help train students' attributions by giving them the messages that we believe in them, that their actions can influence outcomes, and that we are available to support them in their motivation to succeed.

On the other hand, consider the common challenge of dealing with students who seem unmotivated to engage during an instructional activity. If we attribute the lack of engagement in an activity on a fixed quality of the student such as being unmotivated, we are attributing the failure of the lesson to factors beyond our control as teachers. When this happens, what reason is there for us to look for solutions if we believe the problem is outside of our locus of control? However, if we attribute the failure of a lesson to a lack of success in aligning our teaching with our students and the context, we are attributing the outcome to factors that are within our control. When we do this, we tend to keep looking for solutions to increase motivation and engagement.

Again, we challenge readers to hold the assumption that all students have motivation to learn and act in accordance with that assumption.

ACTIVITY 2.3 CRITICAL REFLECTION ACTIVITY

Discuss or write down your assumptions about motivation as

- stable versus unstable,
- internal to the student versus external to the student, or
- controllable versus uncontrollable

What are the implications of those beliefs on your instructional practices?

BELIEFS ABOUT MOTIVATION IN THE CLASSROOM

Now that we have established two key assumptions about motivation, we now turn our attention to beliefs about motivation that are supported by these assumptions. We purposely separate teacher assumptions from their beliefs about teaching and learning, although this is a difficult distinction to make since there is considerable overlap (Pajares, 1992). To us, beliefs are specific theories about the way motivation operates that can be tested, researched, and explored; whereas assumptions are presumptions or unquestioned principles that serve as a basis for the formation of beliefs and how they translate into action.

Although the beliefs teachers hold about teaching and learning may come from a variety of sources—personal educational experience, cultural values, family, social context, teacher training, and popular culture—the beliefs we describe here are based on the research literature outlined in Chapter 1 and set the stage for detailed descriptions of teaching and learning practices that support motivation in Chapters 3 through 6. We chose these specific beliefs because they represent key concepts across several theories of motivation and because they are beliefs that can be translated into action in the classroom.

Belief 1—Motivation Involves Providing the Opportunity for Students to Make Decisions and Express Their Voice in the Classroom

A common complaint by students at various grade levels is that they have little or no voice to make decisions about their learning. For example, the recent 2010 report of the High School Survey of Student Engagement concludes that many adolescents feel that their ideas don't matter. One student wrote, "If this school has taught me anything, it is that my opinion matters not here" (Yazzie-Mintz, 2010, p. 16). Another stated, "This school does not allow students to have a voice in decision-making, even though they say they do" (p. 16). Finally, one student exhorted, "We need teachers to listen to our opinions" (p. 16). Our experiences in classrooms confirm these findings. In general, we notice that classrooms with high levels of motivation tend to give students real and frequent opportunities to make important decisions; in other words, they are autonomy supportive (Jang, Reeve & Deci, 2010; Reeve, Jang, Carrell, Jeon, & Barch, 2004; Stefanou, Perencevich, Dicintio, & Turner, 2004). On the other hand, students tend to be less engaged and energetic in classrooms where they have little autonomy to make decisions.

One of the most robust findings in research on motivation during the past 30 years is that autonomy (particularly autonomy to make decisions) plays a powerful role in building motivation. For example, Self-Determination Theory (Ryan & Deci, 2000) asserts that to feel motivated, individuals need to believe that they play a role in directing their life, along with feelings of competence and relatedness. In other words, an important aspect of motivated activity is the frequent opportunity to make decisions and choose for ourselves. This is extremely important in the classroom. As mentioned earlier, the more students tend to have opportunities to make decisions about their learning, the more motivated they are to engage in learning. In fact, as a way to assess levels of intrinsic motivation, Ryan and Deci (2000) have employed a measure of "free choice" in which participants can continue working on a task even when no external reasons (rewards) exist. They concluded that students who experience autonomy support display more curiosity and seek challenge; whereas, those who are overly controlled lose initiative and show less mastery of conceptual, complex ideas.

Given the positive relationship that often exists between decision making and motivation, it makes sense to provide students with opportunities to make choices and act autonomously in the classroom. Recent research suggests that providing personal and instructional support through classroom organization, classroom procedures, and how work is chosen and evaluated are powerful approaches to enhance motivation (Stefanou et al., 2004) and essential elements of powerful educational practices such as differentiated instruction (Tomlinson, 2008). However, such approaches require us to believe that students are capable of making appropriate decisions and learning from choices that do not turn out as expected. An excellent example of the power of letting students make decisions and giving them time to learn from them can be found in *You Can't Say, You Can't Play*, a wonderful book by Vivian Gussin Paley. In this text, Paley recounts her experience as a kindergarten teacher and how she solved the problem of students excluding other students during playtime activities. Rather than make a decision and solve the problem herself, she guided the class in thinking about the issue and deciding what to do to solve the problem. Paley's confidence and belief that her young students would be able to solve a complex and moral issue in an effective and kind manner is rare and powerfully demonstrates how motivating and effective it can be to let students make important decisions in the classroom.

Belief 2—Motivation Involves Completing Meaningful Work in the Classroom

A refrain from students often heard in some classrooms is "Why does this matter to us?" All of us desire to do work that is important, meaningful, and relevant to our lives and interests. In his book *Labor of Learning*, Sidorkin (2009) decried what he referred to as the "wastebasket economy" of schools. Students produce writing, math problem solutions, book reports, descriptions of historical events, artwork, and lab reports; however, the value that these products contain is often confined to a score or grade from the teacher and a brief glimpse by parents if and when the project is taken home.

In addition to expecting success on a task, Wigfield and Eccles (2000) have shown the importance of task value as another element of motivated activity in the classroom. Beyond feeling capable, students must also see that their work holds some meaning—regarding personal interest, future success, or implications for their daily lives. Believing that classroom tasks hold value has been associated with important educational outcomes such as academic performance and future course taking (Bong, 2004). However, the nature of what learners value may shift as they develop. For example, a child may develop fascination with science as she explores the natural world around her, and may continue to hold that intrinsic value for science. But as an adolescent, she may take an upper-level science course for its value in getting to college or preparing for a career. It is not uncommon to see a shift from pure personal interest to pragmatic, goal-directed interest as learners enter adolescence (Eccles, 2005).

Classroom activities that have direct application to their daily lives hold meaning and are more motivating for students. Recently, one of the authors interviewed an African-American middle school student involved in chronicling the life of a community member who had been involved in the civil rights movement. The biography he produced with his small group of peers was to be displayed in the local museum of history. When asked if he was motivated for this project, he explained that initially when they did the usual classroom readings and activities on the civil rights movement, he was not very motivated. However, once he conducted the interview and realized he was acting as a historian with access to information that the community did not have, his motivation increased sharply.

Meaningfulness and relevance do not always need to involve such long-term projects and efforts. Even simply incorporating students' names and interests into reading and math examples can add some meaningfulness to a routine task. A goal for teachers interested in enhancing relevance should be the habit of integrating connections to students' lives, futures, and communities into the classroom so classroom work has value by virtue of the interest students have in it, its importance to schooling or to society, or its usefulness for meeting future goals.

Belief 3—Motivation Requires Challenging Students at an Appropriate Level and Supporting Them in Being Successful With Those Challenges

Individuals crave optimal challenge. For example, think of a time when you were fully immersed in a task or activity, when time seemed to stand still. On such occasions, what made the task so engrossing? Optimally challenging activities typically match our current level of expertise but require us to stretch our learning and skills to achieve success. In these moments, we usually feel competent enough to complete the challenge or achieve some level of success. Csikszentmihalyi (1990) describes this condition of motivation as "flow"—a time of fully involved, directed focus leading to success in the project. Maintaining this motivational state involves the optimally matched levels of both challenge and skill to avoid anxiety (high challenge and low skill) or boredom (low challenge and high skill). Flow is a state of motivation, cognition, and emotion in which a person is deeply engrossed with little regard for other people, activity, or distractions.

In our research, we have seen that students who sense challenge or demand in their classroom also are more likely to engage in work to improve their competence, show more interest, and are more likely to ask for help (Middleton & Midgley, 2002). Our colleagues have also found similar results when exploring the role of challenge for early adolescents. Meyer and her colleagues (1997) identified "challenge seekers" who had a tolerance for failure, a learning goal, and higher self-efficacy versus "challenge avoiders" who had higher negative affect, lower self-efficacy, and used surface strategies to learn.

Challenge will often only be part of a strong culture of motivation when it is accompanied by a sense of support to meet that challenge. In one study of the social environment of classrooms, teacher social support and peer academic support along with encouragement from the teacher to discuss their work were related to students' use of self-regulatory strategies and engaging in task-related interactions (Patrick, Ryan, & Kaplan, 2007). Teacher support, in addition to promoting interaction and mutual respect, has also been related to positive changes in student motivation and engagement (Ryan & Patrick, 2001).

Despite the motivating effect of meaningful challenges and support for meeting those challenges, it is extremely difficult to design instructional activities that appropriately challenge every student. It is because of this that personalizing and differentiating instruction is so difficult, yet so important. Many forces make it complex for teachers to design tasks that meaningfully challenge all students. For example, large class sizes, prescribed or scripted curricula, limited time, and lack of resources are obstacles many educators contend with when designing compelling learning experiences for students. However, it is important to remember that when students lack enthusiasm during instructional activities, it is usually not because they do not want to be challenged. They do want to be challenged; instead, the task may not be optimally challenging or they may be uncertain of how to succeed at that challenge. Frustration may cause them to give up, mask their failures (e.g., cheat), or act on their frustrations. Alternately, the task might also be too easy. A student may feel that there is little challenge to an activity and, thus, feel little reason to participate or expend effort.

Belief 4—Motivation Involves a Sense of Belonging Through Peer and Student-Teacher Relationships in the Classroom

One aspect of a classroom's motivation climate is a sense of belonging or relationships among peers and between the teacher and students. In fact, certain types of peer relationships, such as group membership, have been found to promote prosocial behavior among students and relate to academic achievement (Wentzel & Caldwell, 2006). Furthermore, positive relationships between teachers and young children have been associated with achievement and have been shown to buffer the negative effects of poor parent-child relationships (O'Connor & McCartney 2007). Among at-risk children, the positive benefits of a good teacher-student relationship can be seen as early as third grade (Baker, 1999). Our understanding that a positive relationship with a teacher may be critical in encouraging success and preventing students from disengaging in school has led many middle and high schools to adopt advisory programs. In general, a positive sense of belonging in school is a critical part of a motivational culture that encourages participation and engagement (Goodenow & Grady, 1993).

Despite what we know about the benefits of positive peer relationships and student-teacher relationships, rather than supporting collaboration, many classrooms and schools adopt practices that may erode relationships. For example, a quick look in many elementary classrooms will reveal posters where students vie to attain the most stickers. At all grade levels, after students receive grades for their work or performance on assessments, they quickly turn to compare their score with their peers. In addition, many high schools continue to sort students by GPA. These are just a few examples of ways schools encourage competition that diminish rather than support relationships. Most teachers do not have difficulty identifying others.

Conventional wisdom might suggest that individuals thrive with competition; however, competitive environments tend to have a negative effect on motivation for many individuals. An examination of 148 studies of competition and cooperation in classrooms found that higher achievement and positive peer relationships were associated with cooperative classrooms rather than competitive or individualistic classrooms (Roseth, Johnson, & Johnson, 2008). Part of the reason for this is that environments that stress individual competition do not promote a sense of belonging within a meaningful community. On the other hand, environments that encourage students to collaborate with others to solve meaningful problems and complete real work, while maintaining a sense of individuality, tend to be places of strong motivation and engagement. This is because students want to be part of a meaningful community doing valued work where they are an important and valued member.

TEACHER STANCE

After defining our assumptions and beliefs about motivation, we now turn our attention to translating those beliefs into action. However, translating beliefs into action can be challenging for many teachers who are accustomed to a particular approach to teaching and strategies for enhancing motivation.

Teacher stance describes the way in which we prepare to act in accordance with our beliefs. It is important to acknowledge that aligning our actions with our beliefs is not always easy. At times we may not know what actions to take or what would even be possible; at other times, we may doubt our beliefs or our capabilities. Many of us believe in ourselves and in our students, but find our daily challenges as teachers and professionals in a complex, ever-changing field to be daunting. This is particularly true in classrooms where we are trying to attain high levels of motivation, engagement, and learning. Teachers cannot always predict how students will respond to any given activity, how the social atmosphere of that particular class of students impacts their motivation, or how the activity is related to the shifting cultural and community context. Therefore, it is important for teachers to take a stance that prepares them to act and adjust in ways that match their beliefs.

Research has shown the strong impact reflective practice can have on teaching (Brookfield, 1995; Farrell, 2004). Reflective practitioners view their teaching as dynamic and open to change. They apply notions of self-regulation to their teaching. The cycle of self regulation (Zimmerman, 1990) includes three main components:

Forethought: Setting goals and making a plan to meet those goals

Monitoring actions: Focusing attention on goals and adjusting to the situation

Evaluation: Self-reflection on what worked and what could be improved

In our conversations with teachers, we've found that the final step—self-reflection—is often sacrificed to more immediate daily concerns. However, it is critical that teachers engaged in self-reflective practice find ways to assess their work in the classroom to develop new strategies and approaches. Missed opportunities or difficult days are easy to brush off, but can become opportunities for improvement.

Some teachers will engage in individual acts of self-reflection by taking notes on lesson plans, collecting and analyzing feedback from students, or journaling. One of our colleagues keeps a "critical incident" notebook that includes descriptions of positive and negative incidents and a brief analysis that can be revisited. Other teachers find ways to include reflective practice within their professional network of colleagues. This can include informal "debriefing" with a teaching friend or colleague to more formal mentoring, peer observations, or critical friends groups. Each of these provides an opportunity for feedback and discussion with knowledgeable peers. Reflective practice may also take place formally as part of action research, with colleagues in a professional learning community or in other forms of professional development. Action research can follow many different models (e.g., Mills, 2010; Pine, 2009) but must include addressing critical classroom issues through a more formal research-based model of posing questions, collecting and analyzing data, and reporting findings. The teacher education program with which we have worked includes a formal action research project for all graduate students. Those students have reported beneficial findings related to both their confidence as new teachers and the quality of their instruction (Finkel & Fletcher, 2002; Middleton, Abrams, & Seaman, 2011).

ACTIVITY 2.4 APPLICATION TO PRACTICE

Focus on the self-regulation cycle described earlier. Follow your actions as a teacher through one cycle. Begin by identifying a belief you have as a teacher.

Teaching Belief	
Corresponding Goal	
Actions Taken	
Reflection on Actions	

Do you see a correspondence between your beliefs and the actions you take? What obstacles did you have to overcome to enact your beliefs? In what ways can you improve the connection between this belief and your actions?

WARM TEACHER STANCE

Taking an open stance toward reflective practice provides a strong basis for translating our beliefs as teachers into practical actions. However, in our conversations with teachers, we have found that not only the initial beliefs, but also the attitudes and approaches they brought into their teaching made a difference. Certainly, we believe that successful implementation of those strategies depends on holding beliefs that correspond to promoting motivation and achievement in the classroom. However, we also believe that teachers' attitudes toward action and change in classroom behaviors will make a difference in their effectiveness. Navigating a river current successfully requires a certain approach to the task. Approaching the river with strength alone and working against the current can be exhausting and self-defeating. It requires skills of observation and adaptability as well as knowing when to paddle hard and when to ride the current. In the classroom, we believe that what we refer to as a WARM stance helps teachers behave in ways that support the two essential assumptions that all students can learn and are motivated to learn. This WARM stance requires teachers to be *Watchful, Adaptable, Reflective, and Modest*. It also prepares teachers to implement the practices and strategies we describe in subsequent chapters more effectively.

Watchfulness

In classrooms where motivation is consistently high, teachers tend to be watchful or observant of what is happening in their classroom. Bringing a watchful stance into the classroom involves being mindful of the experiences and behaviors of students, and relies on being open to how things are, observant of what is occurring, and objective in our interpretations (Siegel, 2010). When teachers are observant, they put themselves in a position to communicate and support the belief that each student has motivation and can succeed. They can be watchful of a variety of classroom qualities such as the way students are working and collaborating, when students are struggling with certain tasks, and how the layout facilitates engagement. In fact, teachers who display this classroom awareness often report higher engagement and fewer discipline problems (Wolfgang, 2005). Teachers can then use the information from this watchful stance to better navigate the motivational energy in the classroom. For example, teachers can encourage students when they falter. They can help students keep focused on their goals and point out their progress. Being alert helps teachers learn if a task is inappropriate as soon as possible. If activities are too easy or too difficult, teachers are able to realize this quickly and make adjustments accordingly. Developing the stance of watchfulness takes time and effort (Schon, 1990) but has the benefit of building student trust and enacting the beliefs regarding student success and motivation that are essential for transforming classroom culture.

Adaptability

When teachers are watchful, they are able to make adjustments to an activity or lesson. However, making adjustments on the fly requires teachers to be adaptable or responsive. Teacher responsiveness in the classroom has been related to a variety of positive outcomes such as students' perception of teacher caring (Teven, 2001) and fewer behavioral challenges (Wanzer & McCroskey, 1994). Adaptability is one quality of prosocial classrooms that are demanding yet supportive of students and are related to learning and positive development (Jennings & Greenberg, 2009) as well as positive teacher-student relationships (Murray & Malmgren, 2005). For example, during a unit on World War II, a teacher we know was having students write a historical fiction narrative as the culminating project. However, when she learned that one of her students had a grandfather who was a World War II veteran, she was willing to modify the project to allow the student to interview her grandfather and write an article on his experiences. The student was not motivated to write a historical narrative but was extremely motivated to interview her grandfather. Because of the teacher's willingness to be adaptable, she was able to modify the task to be more meaningful to the student without compromising her expectations or standards. Such adaptability provides direct support for teachers to enact their beliefs about student success and motivation. Classroom activities are no longer one-size-fits all but can meet the needs, interests, and motives of the students.

Reflectiveness

In addition to being watchful and adaptable, it is also important for teachers to be reflective. As discussed earlier, reflective practice can have a strong impact on teaching (Brookfield, 1995; Farrell, 2004). Most lessons and activities never go exactly as designed. Often, we wish they could have gone better. Therefore, it is important for teachers to take a reflective stance when considering their instructional practices and lesson designs. When teachers take a reflective stance, they become open to new ideas about how their instruction can be improved. Simple steps teachers can take to support a reflective stance toward their practice include journaling, soliciting student feedback, and engaging in more systematic data-driven decision making. By adopting a reflective stance, teachers are able to look critically at the process of translating beliefs into action rather than abandoning beliefs based on occasional failures.

Modesty

Finally, it is critical that teachers remain modest or humble about their work. This statement may seem silly or controversial, but for most of us teaching is a very personal endeavor. In our understanding, modesty does not mean abandoning authority or diminished self-worth but instead embraces the role of reason and research over personal experience and a respect for student perspective (Hare, 2006). Almost all of the teachers we know work extremely hard and invest a great deal of themselves into their lessons and projects. When we put so much of ourselves into our teaching, it is difficult to recognize that our work can continually be improved and developed. It is also a challenge to see beyond our perspective and viewpoint at times. Therefore, a modest stance reminds us to remain open to feedback and suggestions for improvement from students, parents, colleagues, and administrators. The most effective teachers we have worked with constantly seek feedback and strive to improve their pedagogy on a daily basis. When we look beyond our own experience and knowledge, we may be able to find new and innovative ways to support out beliefs that each student is motivated and can learn.

Using this WARM stance, in the next section of the book, we encourage readers to consider particular questions about classroom culture and motivation related to the four beliefs described earlier. To enhance the motivational culture of your classroom, we ask you to consider the following:

1. How do you provide the opportunity for students to make decisions and express their *voice* in the classroom?

2. What opportunities do you provide for students to complete *relevant* and meaningful work in your classroom?

3. How are students being *challenged* at an appropriate level and supported in being *successful* with those challenges?

4. What are you doing to foster a sense of belonging through peer and student-teacher *relationships* in your classroom?

Section I Conclusion

In the first section of the book, we challenged you to consider your understanding of motivation and how your beliefs influence your teaching stance toward students who appear motivated and those who do not. Typically, teachers think about motivation as a quality of individuals or classrooms. However, we provided an alternative in which motivation is seen as a dynamic, interactive force, much like a river current. This metaphor provides a complex view of motivation in which the learner exists, impacts, and is impacted by the social, emotional, and academic context of the classroom. To consider how this view of motivation can help you transform your classroom culture, we provided two underlying assumptions to consider. Specifically, we ask you to consider the notion that all students are capable of learning and all students possess motivation to learn. With these assumptions in mind, we then introduced four beliefs about motivation that are grounded in research. We concluded by describing the WARM stance that prepares teachers to teach in accordance with those beliefs. Section II explores each of these four beliefs more deeply and offers a wide variety of practices and strategies that teachers can integrate into their instruction and assessment.

SECTION II

Classroom Practices and Strategies

INTRODUCTION

Section I of this book described the nature of motivation in the classroom and how our beliefs as teachers influence the ways we access that motivation. Again, we encourage readers to remember that although motivation in the classroom will ebb and flow, it is always there ready to be harnessed. Section II builds on the previous section by describing practices and providing examples of strategies that can help teachers capitalize on and use motivation in the classroom to maximize learning. The next four chapters offer resources that readers can go back to again and again.

Each of the following chapters focuses on an essential element of motivation. Chapter 3 addresses how teachers can tap into motivation by promoting student voice. Chapter 4 provides techniques to help make learning meaningful and relevant. Chapter 5 describes how to scaffold student success on challenging tasks. Chapter 6 describes the importance of fostering positive relationships and explores ways to do this effectively.

Each chapter is divided into multiple sections. Chapters begin with an excerpt from a River View Middle School scenario, which is followed by case study analysis questions to support the application of ideas from each chapter. Next, each chapter defines an element of motivation and describes concrete strategies and practices that teachers can integrate into their instruction. Chapters end with a short assessment tool. Readers are encouraged to use these assessments with their students to determine the extent to which their current practice embodies the concepts focused on in each chapter.

How to Use the Resources in This Section

As previously mentioned, each chapter includes descriptions of concrete practices and strategies that teachers can integrate into their instructional routines to leverage the motivation in their classrooms in support of student learning. It is also important to point out that while each chapter focuses on a single aspect of motivation, and while each of the practices and strategies is informed by research and our experiences, all of the techniques described in the following pages support more than one element of motivation. Therefore, we recommend that readers pick one chapter to focus on at a time and practice applying some of the practices and strategies described before moving on to other chapters.

Finally, another powerful way to work through the ideas and activities in the next four chapters is to do so with other educators. Many schools have book groups, professional learning communities, or critical friends groups where teachers can work together to improve their teaching. Teachers in a book group could select different chapters to focus on and report back to the group. In subsequent meetings, they can share their results, engage in protocols to analyze each other's work, or simply share their individual learning and progress.

Self-Reflection Tool

The surveys on the following pages can help readers identify where to start reading in Section II. This self-reflection tool is designed to provide you with a personal profile of the assets of your classroom and can be used to identify goals for your teaching. To use these tools effectively, we encourage teachers to complete the Teacher Survey first. Next, have students fill out the Student Survey. Once the students have completed the student survey, determine the average score for each of the questions. Once all these data have been collected, examine the results. Use this information to select chapters to focus on: Questions 1 and 2 connect to Chapter 3; Questions 3 and 4 connect to Chapter 4; Questions 5 and 6 go with Chapter 5; and Questions 7 and 8 are addressed in Chapter 6. A summary chart at the end of the surveys will help you set your goals and choose where to begin this section.

It is important to note that these are very general assessments of the perception of motivational qualities of your classroom. Their purpose is to begin the reflective process, not to evaluate you, your students, or your classroom. The survey questions we provide on the following pages were designed for a general audience of teachers and students. You may want to adapt the questions to be more appropriate for the subject area you teach or for the age of your students. They are intended to be a starting point for you and should be adjusted as necessary to provide the most benefit to your process of reflection.

MOTIVATION IN THE CLASSROOM

TEACHER SURVEY

Use the following scale to answer how often each statement is true for you.

1 = Rarely 2 = Seldom 3 = Occasionally 4 = Routinely 5 = Always

1. I give students opportunities to make decisions in the classroom.

    1   2   3   4   5

2. I give students choices during lessons or activities.

    1   2   3   4   5

3. I make sure students understand what they are supposed to learn in each lesson or activity.

    1   2   3   4   5

4. I make sure students understand why each lesson or activity is important.

    1   2   3   4   5

5. I make sure that tasks and activities are not too hard and not too easy for each student.

    1   2   3   4   5

6. I make sure all students can succeed on all tasks and activities.

    1   2   3   4   5

7. Activities and lessons in the class allow students to get to know their classmates better.

    1   2   3   4   5

8. Activities and lessons in the class allow me to build positive relationships with students.

    1   2   3   4   5

Motivation in the Classroom

Student Survey

Use the following scale to answer how often each statement is true for you.

1 = Rarely 2 = Seldom 3 = Occasionally 4 = Routinely 5 = Always

1. The teacher gives me opportunities to make decisions in the classroom.

   1   2   3   4   5

2. The teacher gives me choices during lessons or activities.

   1   2   3   4   5

3. I understand what I am supposed to learn from each lesson or activity.

   1   2   3   4   5

4. I understand why each lesson or activity is important.

   1   2   3   4   5

5. The tasks and activities the teachers give me are not too hard and not too easy.

   1   2   3   4   5

6. I can succeed on tasks my teacher gives me.

   1   2   3   4   5

7. Activities and lessons in the class allow me to get to know my classmates better.

   1   2   3   4   5

8. Activities and lessons in the class allow me to get to know my teacher(s) better.

   1   2   3   4   5

Your survey results can be summarized next. Those topics with higher numbers are likely to be existing motivational assets of your classroom. The areas with the lowest scores may be areas to begin your exploration of classroom strategies and instructional tools in the chapters in Section II of this book.

Survey Scores

Teacher Survey		Student Survey		
Q1 +	Q2 +	Q1 +	Q2 =	TOTAL—**STUDENT VOICE**
___ +	___ +	___ +	___ =	_____
Teacher Survey		Student Survey		
Q3 +	Q4 +	Q3 +	Q4 =	TOTAL—**MEANINGFUL LEARNING**
___ +	___ +	___ +	___ =	_____
Teacher Survey		Student Survey		
Q5 +	Q6 +	Q5 +	Q6 =	TOTAL—**PROMOTING CHALLENGE WITH SUCCESS**
___ +	___ +	___ +	___ =	_____
Teacher Survey		Student Survey		
Q7 +	Q8 +	Q7 +	Q8 =	TOTAL—**POSITIVE RELATIONSHIP**
___ +	___ +	___ +	___ =	_____

	TOTAL
Chapter 3 Promoting Student Voice	_____
Chapter 4 Designing Meaningful Learning Tasks	_____
Chapter 5 Promoting Challenge With Success	_____
Chapter 6 Building Positive Relationships Around Learning	_____

3

Promoting
Student Voice

As the River View Middle School students entered their third period class, Mr. Jackson asked for a volunteer to pass out a small packet to the students. Once the students had settled into their seats and had the packets on their desks, Mr. Jackson asked for their attention.

"Good morning everyone. I hope you are having a good day so far. You might recall from yesterday's class that we will be starting a new unit in a couple of weeks. The next unit will focus on plate tectonics. Who has an idea of what plate tectonics is about?"

Mr. Jackson scans the room and sees a few students raise their hands. "Great, some of you know a little bit about it. Wonderful. What I would like you to do now is to review the materials I have put in front of you. The packet on your desk is my proposal for the unit of study on plate tectonics. As you have done before, I would like you to take the feedback sheet at the back and give me your thoughts about the unit. As always, I want to know what is clear and what is not clear. I love suggestions that might make the unit better. You may review the packet and give feedback by yourself, or you can work with one other partner. You may also find a comfortable place to read and write your feedback—you do not need to sit at your desks. Okay—go to work! Come see me if you have any questions!"

In short order, the students find partners and settle down to read. After a few minutes, Becky and Ron walk up to Mr. Jackson. "Mr. Jackson, Ron and I are interested in doing one of the alternate challenges in the plate tectonics unit. Can we talk about that?"

Mr. Jackson smiles. "Sure thing. Let's go sit at my desk and we can talk about it."

CASE STUDY ANALYSIS QUESTIONS—SET 3.1

This part of the case study highlights the powerful role student voice plays in leveraging motivation. Consider the following questions before we explore student voice more deeply and how to promote it in the classroom.

1. How would you define student voice?

2. What strategies does Mr. Jackson use to promote student voice or to give students ownership in the classroom?

3. What types of choices do the students have in this short excerpt? How do you think the students feel about the choices they are given? What other opportunities for choice do you see?

4. What is the purpose of asking the students to give feedback on a unit of study before it is implemented? How do you think the students feel about having this opportunity?

5. What do you think will happen during the discussion Becky and Ron will have with Mr. Jackson?

6. To what extent do you promote student voice in your classroom?

7. What kinds of choices do you give to students?

8. To what extent are students involved in decisions about lesson and unit design?

9. What types of decisions are students allowed to make during instructional activities?

10. How are students involved in decision making after a lesson or unit has been completed?

A powerful way to harness motivation to learn in any classroom is to encourage *student voice*. *Voice* refers to the extent to which students have the "opportunity to influence decisions that will shape their lives and those of their peers either in or outside of school settings" (Toshalis & Nakkula, 2012, p. 23). In general, when students are given autonomy to make decisions that relate to their learning, their motivation to learn and their engagement in learning activities increase (Black & Deci, 2000).

Consider your learning experiences as a student, as well as your "motivation for teaching." Most teachers tend to be more motivated when they have significant ownership of instructional decisions in their classrooms. How much motivation would you have if your school or district administrators made all of the instructional decisions for you? Now think about this from the students' perspective. In general, students will be more motivated if they perceive some ownership or voice in their learning. This does not mean we relinquish the reins to the students; rather, it means we include them in the teaching and learning process. This is true for students at any grade level.

The purpose of this chapter is to provide teachers with concrete strategies to encourage student voice. The chapter begins by describing a continuum of ways to include students in decision making. This continuum consists of three broad practices: offering choices, soliciting feedback and input from students, and collaborating with students on content and instruction. The remainder of the chapter provides strategies to promote student voice related to each practice on the continuum.

PRACTICES AND STRATEGIES THAT PROMOTE STUDENT VOICE

In this chapter, we describe three practices for promoting student voice. To help readers understand the differences between these practices we have placed the practices on a continuum (See Figure 3.1). The first section of Figure 3.1 focuses on choice. Choices can be provided during any phase of teaching and learning. Choices begin to give students some ownership of decision making (Katz & Assor, 2007). The second section emphasizes student feedback to teachers on instruction and assessment. This gives students even greater voice in the classroom, and it uses students' insights about teaching and learning to help shape learning activities (Hattie, 2009). The third part of the continuum addresses the practice of giving students opportunities to collaborate or codesign instructional lessons, units, and projects. At this level of practice, students are valued as codevelopers of the curriculum. As Figure 3.1 illustrates, as teacher practices shift from providing students with choice to collaborating with students on instruction, students' perception of autonomy increases as does their motivation.

Offering Choice

A simple, yet powerful way to promote student voice in the classroom is to give students choice. However, not all types of choices will motivate all students. Nor will all students perceive

Figure 3.1   Teacher Practices of Promoting Student Voice

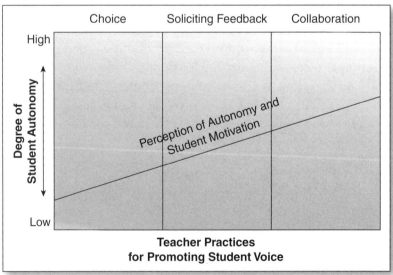

specific choices the same way (Iyengar & Lepper, 2000; Sethi, 1998). For example, in an English Language Arts class, some students will embrace the opportunity to choose from many options during a journaling activity; other students will prefer a more limited set of selections. Often the reason for this is that some students can become paralyzed with too many choices. Students may also worry about making a wrong choice when there are many items to select from (O'Connor & Stravynski, 1997). In such situations, a happy medium can be accomplished by providing one or two options and having an open-ended choice.

One effective approach to providing choice is to give students a range of simple choices. Although such choices have a limited impact on instruction, they have a powerful impact on students' perceptions of autonomy (Katz & Assor, 2007). Therefore, when designing activities and lessons, we encourage teachers to use what we refer to as the 4WH framework to create opportunities for choice during any given unit, lesson, or activity. This framework encourages teachers to ask *who, what, when, where,* and *how* questions.

Who will students work with?

When activities require students to work in groups, giving them some choice about whom they get to work with may tap into their motivation. Teachers may be concerned that disruptions will occur when students sit with their friends. Some mitigate this by allowing students to pick one or two friends they would like to work with. The teacher then takes these recommendations into consideration when making work groups.

What content will students work with?

When activities are designed to provide opportunities to practice specific skills, students appreciate being able to select the topics or the content that they can work with. This helps to give greater purpose or meaning to a task. For example, if a teacher wants students to practice comprehension skills, he or she may allow them to select from a list of short stories or interesting informational texts to find something that will appeal to their interests. Another example comes from elementary school where we have seen teachers allow students to add to their own vocabulary lists. In addition to words assigned by the teacher, students are encouraged to find additional vocabulary terms from their readings to learn and study.

When will students need to complete specific tasks?

Many projects do not require students to complete a task or solve a problem in a linear fashion. Giving students flexibility about when they do parts of a task may encourage higher levels of engagement because it gives them a sense of control and may allow them to regulate the difficulty of the task. A good example of this occurs when students are working on writing work. Although the writing process has clear stages, writing is not a linear process. For example, if students are working on a lab report, some students may need to work on revising, while others may need to be focused on editing.

Where will students work?

Students do not always need to work at their desks. For example, one teacher we work with noticed that the students were getting restless during independent reading in class. They became more motivated and less fidgety when the teacher allowed them to find a comfortable place to read. Some student chose to remain at their desks. Others crawled under the desks. The rest found comfortable places elsewhere. Even simple choices like this can give students a meaningful sense of control.

How will students complete a given task?

Many tasks we ask students to complete do not need to be completed in the same manner. A math teacher we know gives students the option of finding creative ways to solve math problems. She has commented that she continues to be impressed with the innovative ways students attempt to solve equations and other mathematical problems. Choices like this honor divergent ways of thinking and in doing so help promote strong feelings of competence in students.

There are additional elements to consider when giving students options. One important consideration is the amount of choice. Another is the meaningfulness of choices. As an important element of any activity, choice can encourage students to harness their motivation. However, as mentioned earlier, not all students will react to choices in the same way. For some students, choices may help them tap into their motivation; for others the choices may become a barrier.

Number of choices. There is no magic number regarding how many options to give students when providing them with choices. However, a good rule of thumb is to give students a limited amount of choice. That being said, some students prefer to have many options, whereas other students will become very anxious or 'paralyzed' when there are too many options (O'Connor & Stravynski, 1997). Therefore, we encourage teachers to hedge their bets. For example, when assigning a research project, a social studies teacher might provide students with a short list of topics, but also allow students to propose their own topic.

Meaningful choices. As the 4WH questions demonstrate, choices do not always need to be substantive to be motivating; they just need to be meaningful to students (Assor, Kaplan, & Rotj, 2002). Although the concept of meaningfulness is explored more fully in the next chapter, a common mistake many teachers make is believing that only important choices have a positive relationship with motivation. Oftentimes, this is not true. For example, if students are working on a project in groups, giving them the choice of working at their desks or on the floor can tap into their motivation. Encouraging students to make informed choices is also helpful. On some occasions it makes a lot of sense to allow students to adjust their choice or change their mind once they realize they might have made a poor decision with a recent choice.

Equal choices. Perhaps the most important element to consider when giving students choices is to make sure that all choices are equal when expecting students to demonstrate learning at a specific level of rigor. On many occasions, we have seen teachers give students a list of options to show what they have learned but the choices were uneven. For example, we once observed a science teacher who wanted students to demonstrate their learning on plate tectonics. Included on a long list of choices were options to write a rap song, create a poster, draw a picture, or write a poem. While these choices had a wide variety of appeal to students, they did not demand equal levels of rigor. As a result, this made it very difficult for the teacher to validly assess the learning.

In sum, choices are a useful way to promote voice in the classroom, but doing so is not always straightforward. Different students will not always perceive the same choices in the same way. Whereas one type of choice may seem to tap into the motivation of one student, another student may seem to be demotivated by it. Therefore, when beginning to provide choice, keep the options simple and limited. If a teacher wants to expand the number of options or provide students with weightier decisions, it is important to know the students well and to monitor their reactions so that adjustments can be made in a timely manner (Hattie, 2012).

Soliciting Instructional Feedback

Another group of strategies for promoting student voice and involving students in decision making is to solicit student feedback and input about instructional activities before and after learning. Feedback is a very powerful strategy for promoting student voice in any learning context (Pollock, 2012). In education, feedback refers to information about the effectiveness of a process or procedure. Although teachers frequently give students feedback about their learning, it is less common to see teachers requesting student feedback about their practice (Hattie, 2012). Encouraging students to provide information about instruction promotes increased ownership over learning experiences. However, for feedback to harness student motivation, it is essential that students perceive that their input is valued.

There is a common misperception that feedback is something only given by teachers to students. Giving students timely feedback about their learning is an essential practice, and we discuss it in greater detail in subsequent chapters. However, feedback is not a one-way street. In our experience, teachers who are best at drawing on motivation and supporting learning routinely seek feedback about their planning and teaching (Hattie, 2012). Often, the best sources of feedback are not administrators, mentors, or colleagues, all who have little time to be in classrooms. Rather, it is the students themselves who are present each day that have valuable insights into planning, teaching, and learning.

What type of feedback should teachers request? In short, feedback can be requested about any aspect of learning, teaching, or assessment. Table 3.1 displays a variety of questions teachers can ask to solicit student input and feedback.

Questions such as the ones in Table 3.1 can be asked throughout the instructional process. Next are four strategies teachers can use at different phases of instruction to solicit feedback from students. These include the following: The Green Light Survey, Entrance Tickets, Fist-to-Five, and Exit Tickets. All of these strategies can be easily adapted to any grade level and content area.

Green Light Survey

An excellent time to begin requesting feedback from students is before a lesson or unit has begun. The Green Light Survey is a strategy we have developed to solicit student input after a unit has been designed and before it has been implemented. The survey can be found at the end of this chapter and should be given to students before a unit begins. This survey encourages students to review a unit or assignment in

Table 3.1   Questions to Solicit Student Input and Feedback

Feedback About Learning Objectives and Goals
Was the purpose of the lesson clear?
Do you know what you were expected to learn?
Do you know what skills you were expected to practice?
Was it clear how you were expected to demonstrate your learning?
Feedback About Relevance of Work
How meaningful was the content or skills you were expected to learn?
How well did activities help you learn?
How clearly did activities connect to other schoolwork?
How clearly did activities connect to work outside of school?
Feedback About Challenge and Support
Was the work too easy or too hard? If so, what could be done to improve this?
How likely were your chances of succeeding or completing the work?
What could be done to improve chances of success in the future?
Feedback About Lesson Design
Which activities during today's lesson were the most helpful?
Which activities were the least useful?
What was the most difficult? Why?
Was there the right amount of balance between group work and individual work? If not, what could be done to improve this in the future?
Feedback About Learning
What did you learn?
What continues to be confusing?
What questions do you still have?

advance, and it gives them the opportunity to offer suggestions to improve it. Some teachers post instructional materials on the classroom or teacher's website before a unit or project begins and ask students to post feedback and comments.

Entrance Tickets

Entrance tickets are another strategy teachers can use at the beginning of a lesson or class to gather information from students to inform instruction and help a teacher make adjustments to a lesson plan (Brookhart, 2010). When using this strategy, teachers give students a small number of questions at the beginning of a class or lesson. Common questions that teachers put on entrance tickets include questions about homework, what they feel they need to practice or work on in class, and what they would like to accomplish by the end of the lesson. Table 3.2 provides some examples of entrance tickets that can be used at different grade levels. Feel free to create your own questions.

Fist-To-Five

Fist-To-Five is a quick and simple strategy to solicit student input during a lesson (Fletcher, 2002). The purpose of this strategy is to collect information from students about instruction and learning as it is taking place. When using this strategy, teachers ask questions that students can answer on a scale

Table 3.2 Sample Entrance Ticket Questions

Elementary	Middle & High School
What did we do yesterday?	What did we focus on yesterday?
What was hard?	What were the most challenging parts of your recent work?
What was easy?	What was the least challenging part of your recent work?
What could we do today to help you learn?	What should our goals for today be?

from zero to five. Here are some examples of questions teachers can ask.

How many more minutes do you need to finish what you are working on?

How clear is the work?

To what extent are you on track to accomplish your work?

How well is your group working together?

Teachers who use Fist-To-Five on a regular basis may want to display a poster with information to help students know what number to select. This is particularly helpful in elementary and middle school classrooms. Figure 3.2 provides an example for a poster. Students can use this poster as a reference when teachers ask Fist-To-Five questions.

Figure 3.2

Fist-To-Five		
5 Fingers	=	Very Clear, Great, Extremely Well
4 Fingers	=	Clear, Good, Well
3 Fingers	=	Not Sure, Undecided
2 Fingers	=	Clear, Bad, Not so Good
1 Finger	=	Very Unclear, Terrible, Poor
Fist	=	I Have No Clue

Exit Tickets

Another opportunity to solicit feedback is immediately after an activity, a lesson, or unit has been completed. The Exit Ticket is a strategy that is very similar to an Entrance Ticket and can be used at the end of a class or lesson to receive feedback about instruction and learning. Exit tickets should be very short surveys that can be completed on an index card or sticky note. They are often limited to a short list of questions about the day's instruction and activities. On the following pages are examples of a Green Light Survey and an Entrance/Exit Ticket.

Green Light Survey

Directions

We will soon be starting a new unit of instruction. Please review all the materials for the unit and respond to the questions. I highly value your thoughts and opinions. Your feedback will be used to make any changes to the unit before we begin.

How clear is the purpose of the unit? What will you learn? How you will show me that you learned it?

What do you like? What do you not like?

Summarize the steps of what you will be asked to do. Is there enough time? Too much time?

How does this work connect to what we have been studying and learning recently?

How challenging do you think this unit will be? Where might the work be too easy or too hard?

What additional questions or suggestions do you have to make this unit a more valuable learning experience?

What is missing?

Exit Ticket

Directions

Please respond to the following questions thoughtfully. Your responses will help design upcoming lessons and activities. Your feedback will also help me improve the lesson for future students.

What did you learn today? Was it what you expected to learn?

What, if anything, do you still need help with? Or what still confuses you?

What questions do you have about what you learned or what took place today?

Any additional comments or suggestions about today's work?

Collaborative Learning Practices

A more intensive approach to promoting student voice is to invite students to collaborate with the teacher(s) and possibly other students to design and implement learning tasks. As Toshalis and Nakkula (2012) point out, when students begin to collaborate with teachers, they assume much greater ownership of their learning. This type of collaboration encourages students to work with teachers and peers to set goals, coplan, make decisions about processes and strategies, and ultimately accept responsibility for products and learning outcomes. It may also include coguiding group processes and helping to facilitate activities.

A key distinction between a collaborative learning approach and those described previously is that when students collaborate with the teacher and classmates they share responsibility for determining choices and making decisions. They also take a key role in collecting and responding to data and feedback that are collected. Whereas providing choice and soliciting feedback encourage students to participate in parts of the decision-making process, both approaches emphasize the teacher as the primary decision maker. On the other hand, when teachers encourage students to collaborate, they invite students to take ownership of learning to a much greater degree. For many students, this increase in responsibility and ownership allows students to tap into currents of motivation that are often more powerful and enduring.

Students can be invited to collaborate in any phase of teaching and learning. Some teachers who are effective at creating highly engaged classrooms collaborate with students to establish rules at the beginning of the year. One effective practice of collaboration is democratic governance, where teachers and students work together to create classroom rules and procedures. Another collaborative practice includes collaborative learning models in instruction like project-based learning and service learning.

Democratic Governance

An important element of decision making in all learning contexts are decisions related to norms, rules, procedures, and policies. Although most schools have preexisting rules and policies, there is still a great deal of leeway for classrooms to establish additional norms and procedures. In most of the high motivation classrooms we have witnessed, teachers work with the students to establish and maintain democratic practices. This is true at any grade level.

A wonderful example of democratic practice in an early elementary classroom can be found in Vivian Gussin Paley's (1992) *You Can't Say, You Can't Play,* which was referred to earlier. As a teacher of young primary students, Paley noticed that some students would often exclude other students from participating in activities and games. Like most teachers, Paley recognized that this was wrong and saw a powerful opportunity for learning. However, where most of us might have created a rule prohibiting students from excluding others, Paley took a more democratic approach. She shared the problem with her students and worked with them to solve it collectively. Her narrative recounts the collaborative and democratic process she used to engage her students in understanding and solving the problem together. Based on Paley's account, the students were highly motivated to explore and address the issue. As a result, even though the children involved were very young, Paley describes how they came to deeply understand a complex social issue. Eventually, Paley's students created and agreed on a rule for the classroom that encouraged kindness and inclusion.

Collaborative Learning

Perhaps the most comprehensive approach to involving students in decision making occurs when teachers plan instructional activities with students. Such collaborative learning occurs when students are leaders or coleaders in the instructional process (Chiu, 2000). This is different from cooperative learning, which refers to types of activities where students work cooperatively with other students on discrete tasks in groups (Slavin, 1995).

There are a variety of approaches to collaborative teaching and learning that are designed around common principles. Two popular models that are grounded in the type of collaborative learning we describe here are project-based learning and service learning. While there are differences between each model, both approaches involve teachers working with students to identify a problem or need in a local setting or community, planning a solution to the problem or addressing the need in a way that will also help students master important skills and content knowledge, implementing the project or work, and finally assessing it.

Project-Based Learning

Project-based learning, which is sometimes referred to as problem-based learning (Strobel & van Barneveld, 2009; Walker & Leary, 2009), is a teaching and learning approach that focuses on encouraging students to apply knowledge and skills to solve real-world problems (Thomas, 2000). Within this approach, students develop knowledge by exploring and researching realistic problems. Often, students work in pairs or groups with teachers functioning as coaches or facilitators. In this way, students are given increased control over their learning (Barron & Darling-Hammond, 2008).

Implementing project-based learning, while having the potential to be highly rewarding, can also be challenging. This is why we have placed it at the far end of the continuum for promoting student voice. Nonetheless, various researchers have identified essential characteristics of effective project-based learning (e.g., Ertmer & Simmons, 2005). One characteristic is identifying a driving question that is of interest to students. Another is ensuring that students have access to and the ability to locate helpful resources. Third, students must be encouraged to take ownership of the problem. As mentioned earlier, project-based learning is an approach where students take significant responsibility for the learning.

Service Learning

Service learning is much like project-based learning (Eyler & Giles, 1999). Within a service-learning approach, students and teachers work together to identify and solve real-world problems situated within specific community contexts. Again, teachers function as coaches and facilitators to help students (1) identify problems or challenges that are of interest and importance to students, (2) locate and gather resources, (3) plan and coordinate activities to learn more about and address the problem, and (4) present, publish, or communicate products and results to appropriate audiences. A key emphasis of service learning is solving problems that provide a service or support to a community that students value. As a result, the products and outcomes of service-learning projects often have a high level of meaning and relevance for students (see Chapter 4).

One simple example of an effective service-learning project comes from one of our colleagues. As an English teacher from a high school in Maine, she worked with students to identify an issue in the school that would require the students to engage in research, reading, writing, and presenting findings and recommendations to a real audience. After investigating and analyzing a variety of student proposals, the class decided to address a problem related to laptops. As part of a recent state initiative in Maine, all students received their own laptop. However, there were frequent complaints from students, teachers, and parents that laptops were becoming more of a distraction than an aid to learning. Based on their initial inquiry, students generated the following driving question: *Are laptops an aid or hindrance to student learning?*

To better understand the problem, the students explored current research on the benefits of laptop use, interviewed teachers, administrators, and students to better understand the situation and actual set of problems related to laptop use in high school. The result was a report and presentation to the school board on a set of policy proposals around the appropriate use of laptops. After the presentation, students were asked what they thought about the laptop project. Many students commented that this project was one of the hardest, yet most meaningful and memorable academic experiences they had in high school. Students also commented that even though the project was very rigorous, the fact that they truly owned the work helped to make it highly motivating.

CHAPTER SUMMARY

As mentioned earlier in the chapter, students' perception of their autonomy is a powerful component of motivation, and promoting student voice is an effective method for tapping this aspect of motivation. Within our metaphor where motivation is like the current of a river, student perceptions are oars or paddles that allow students to connect to the energy below the surface. Just as oars function as levers, student perception does more than connect to the energy, it allows students to leverage this energy and use it to propel them toward their goals. In sum, if we want to leverage motivation to support student learning, then students must feel as if they have a meaningful role in decision making. This is true for students at any grade level.

It is important to point out at this time a common concern of giving too much control to students. Some teachers worry that involving students too deeply in decision-making processes can adulterate or undermine learning. This is an understandable concern. However, it is important to point out that regardless of the level of involvement students have in decision making, the teacher is still responsible for ensuring that students learn essential skills and content. Including students in the process or elements of the process of teaching and learning does not require abdicating professional obligations. To return to the metaphor of whitewater rafting, the guide has ultimate control over the raft. It is the guide's choice to determine how much impact the paddlers will have on the course the raft takes. An experienced guide can bring a boat through rapids, or she can let the paddlers do the work. As anyone who has ever rafted knows, the best experiences occur when the paddlers' actively participate in the journey. The same is true with learning.

CHAPTER WRAP-UP ACTIVITY

The following tool is designed to help teachers determine the extent to which their current practices encourage student voice. This tool can be used in a variety of ways. Teachers can complete the tool on their own to determine areas of relative strength and weaknesses. They can also give the tool to students. Since student voice is rooted in their *perception* of autonomy and decision making, the tool provides valuable data about how students' perceive tasks and activities in the learning context. In fact, it is important for teachers to determine if student perceptions differ from theirs.

Once a teacher has completed the survey with students, he or she can analyze the results. Based on the data, a teacher can decide where to focus on improving practices of fostering student voice. If results indicate that a teacher rarely provides choice, solicits input, or engages in collaborative practice, it is probably best to focus on increasing strategies for providing choices. On the other hand, a teacher may find that she frequently gives students choices, but rarely engages in the other practices. In this instance, it makes sense to increase strategies for soliciting input and feedback from students. Teachers who regularly provide choice and solicit feedback are likely ready to embrace democratic and collaborative practices of learning.

Survey Questions

Providing Choice

How frequently are students provided with opportunities to make choices?

Routinely	Frequently	Occasionally	Rarely	Never
1	2	3	4	5

Describe the typical kinds of choices provided to students, if any:

Soliciting Student Input and Feedback

How frequently are students asked to give feedback about lessons, units, projects, and assessments?

Routinely	Frequently	Occasionally	Rarely	Never
1	2	3	4	5

And how frequently is this feedback used and taken into consideration by the teacher?

Routinely	Frequently	Occasionally	Rarely	Never
1	2	3	4	5

Describe ways feedback is requested, if any.

Inviting Collaboration

How frequently are students encouraged to collaborate in designing classroom rules, procedures, and/or instructional activities?

Routinely	Frequently	Occasionally	Rarely	Never
1	2	3	4	5

Describe ways the teacher invites collaboration with students, if any.

4

Designing Meaningful Learning Tasks

The students in Mrs. Sullivan's class fidgeted in their seats as they waited for the bell to ring. It was clear they were excited. They had been waiting to start the River View Inn Green Project for weeks. It was an interdisciplinary project between their English, science, and math teachers.

When the bell rang, Mrs. Sullivan immediately began to explain the project. She told them that the main objective of the project was to redesign one of the rooms at the River View Inn, a two-hundred-year-old historic getaway. The project would begin with students dividing into small teams. Each team would be given a small budget. With the small budget, their task was to develop a proposal to redesign the room to embody ecofriendly principles they had been learning in science. The proposals would be given to the owner of the River View Inn in a week.

The group with the winning proposal would lead the rest of the class in putting the proposal into action. This would include buying and selecting materials, developing written materials to display in the room, and finally helping to renovate the room itself. Mrs. Sullivan told the students that they could request who they worked with on their proposals but that she would have the final say about who worked with whom.

CASE STUDY ANALYSIS QUESTION–SET 4.1

This case study highlights the importance of meaningfulness for tapping into student motivation to learn. Consider the following before we explore meaningfulness more deeply.

1. What makes a learning activity meaningful for you?

2. What strategies does Mrs. Sullivan use to help make the River View Inn Green Project meaningful?

3. What parts of the project do you think students would find meaningful?

4. How do you think the project will help students apply concepts and skills being learned and studied in English, science, and mathematics?

5. Consider a learning experience in the past that was meaningful and highly motivating for your students. What made the activity meaningful? Was it meaningful for all students?

6. Based on your teaching experience, what do you think are important characteristics that make learning meaningful?

MEANINGFUL LEARNING

In Chapter 3, we learned about the importance of student voice in the classroom and how supporting autonomy helps teachers harness motivation. Another essential element that helps teachers tap into student motivation is the meaningfulness of learning activities. Most of us probably would recognize meaningful learning when we experience it. In short, as individuals we tend to find activities to be meaningful if we decide that we *want* to engage in them (Eccles, 2009). Thus, it is important to consider factors that encourage students to want to engage in classroom lessons and allow teachers to tap into this motivation.

As we mentioned briefly in Chapter 1, one reason students might engage in learning activities is if they perceive them to be valuable (Wigfield & Eccles, 2002). Since students tend to value many things, there are a variety of ways to integrate meaningfulness into activities and lessons. Based on the work of Eccles and colleagues, we categorize value into three groups: learning tasks that are interesting, those that are useful, and those that have social value (Downey, Eccles, & Chatman, 2005; Downey, Eccles, & Chatman, 2005). We describe these in greater detail next.

Interest

When students find an activity to be interesting and enjoyable, they perceive intrinsic worth in what they are doing (Csikszentmihalyi, 2005). Most teachers dream of having all of their students be intrinsically motivated to engage in classroom learning, but often this is not the case. However, although some students may not have individual interest in what is being learned, teachers can leverage situational interest and guide it into a deeper and more sustained interest over time.

In recent years, researchers have identified how teachers can harness student motivation by creating or tapping into situational interest. Similar to the "catch and hold" process described earlier, Hidi and Renninger (2006) present a four-phase model that can help teachers create or capitalize on what educators often refer to as the "teachable moment." We consider these four phases to be much like the phases of building a fire: lighting a spark, building the flame, feeding the fire, and maintaining the embers. We describe each phase and suggest strategies for implementing them.

The first phase of building interest is much like lighting a fire; it all begins with an initial spark or hook (Mitchell, 1993). During this phase, teachers create or take advantage of a situation that captures or ignites students' interest and attention. These situations can be triggered by an orchestrated surprise, an engaging problem, or a situation that elicits powerful emotions. During this initial phase it is essential for a teacher to promote positive feelings or a sense of empowerment, as well as encourage students to engage in activities that relate to the situation at hand. Some strategies that teachers can use to spark situational interest include, but need not be limited to, taking advantage of natural situations that arise and can be integrated into learning (see Figure 4.1), creating engaging scenarios, using videos, or designing problems that will pique student interest.

The second phase of building interest is similar to that of building a flame once it has been ignited. Once a fire has been lit, care must be taken to slowly build the flame. If a person adds too much or too little fuel, the flame will vanish, much like students' motivation if their interest is not nurtured. Once a situation has captured students' interest, teachers must design activities that will help students see value in activities related to the situation that captured their interest. Some strategies teachers can use to build on initial interest include setting short-term goals, providing additional information, setting a challenge, or designing an experiment.

An important element of the first two phases of building interest that teachers should keep in mind is the role they play in helping students develop foundational knowledge related

Figure 4.1   Four-Phase Model of Interest Building

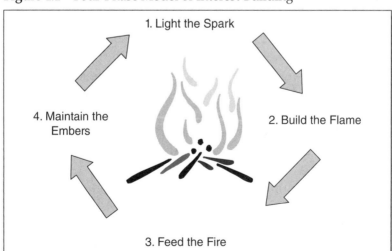

1. Light the Spark

4. Maintain the Embers

2. Build the Flame

3. Feed the Fire

to the topic at hand. By lighting a spark or hooking students' interest and building on it, teachers are creating experiences that will build a knowledge base that students can draw on during the third and fourth phases of the process.

The third phase of building interest is much like feeding a fire once a flame has been established. This is where situational interest can shift into a deeper and more personal interest in the topic or activity. Teachers can encourage this shift by continuing to promote positive feelings about the learning and by continuing to help students build knowledge and see value in what they are doing. Activities that teachers can use to feed the growing student interest often involve students applying what they have already learned.

The final step is much akin to what happens after a fire has been well established. Embers form that will last a long time as long as they are not ignored and left alone for too long. All a teacher needs to do is maintain the embers. Once this happens, it is easy to tap into the energy that exists and rekindle the fire. Thus, at this point of interest building, students have developed personal interest and will often take ownership of activity and learning. What teachers need to do is provide opportunities for students to continue applying the knowledge and skills they have learned to new situations.

ACTIVITY 4.1

On the next two pages there is an example of a teacher who used all four phases to build interest in a rural, elementary school class. As you read the example on the following page, try to identify each of the four phases of the interest-building process and explain what strategies the teacher is using to build interest in this situation. Consider how you might approach similar situations that arise in your context. We encourage readers to do this activity with colleagues and to compare their thoughts and responses.

(Continued)

(Continued)

Mr. Kobe is an elementary teacher in a small school in New England. One day he observed that his students were very upset when they came back from recess. The students were annoyed because part of the playground had been placed off-limits due to erosion during a series of recent storms and it was not safe for play.

Mr. Kobe quickly recognized that this incident provided an opportunity for the students to explore a problem and learn what was causing the playground to erode. He saw many connections to the science, mathematics, and language arts curriculum. Therefore, when the students began complaining about the playground closure, he began asking questions about why the problem might have occurred, what could possibly be done to prevent it from happening in the future, and also what the students could do to help solve the problem.

Most of the students became even more interested when they began to believe they could help repair the playground. Therefore, Mr. Kobe designed some activities that encouraged the students to investigate the issue. They worked in groups to research concepts like soil erosion and methods for preventing it. Based on what they learned, they then went to the playground to analyze the situation to better understand what was happening with the soil erosion on the school's property.

Next, with Mr. Kobe's help, the students contacted the local watershed alliance to develop plans to fix the problem and prevent erosion in the future. The students proposed solutions and the watershed alliance group selected the best proposals and worked with the students to implement and build soil prevention strategies. Students were so engaged in this project, they presented their work to the school board. The students expressed a desire to look for other problems they could solve on the school site.

Usefulness

Although most teachers want all their students to be intrinsically motivated, it is not always possible. A common misperception among many teachers is that all activities need to have intrinsic value for students to find the learning meaningful (Olsson, 2008; Sansone & Harackiewicz, 2000). This is not the case. Teachers can also tap into student motivation by connecting what takes place in the classroom to things students perceive to have extrinsic worth (Ryan & Deci, 2006). Three strategies for doing this are (1) to link student work and learning to their goals, (2) to design authentic tasks that simulate the kinds of work students may encounter later, and (3) to connect students with experts or more knowledgeable individuals in the field.

A few anecdotes illustrate the power of helping students perceive the usefulness of what they are doing and learning. One story comes from an individual who was one of our former students. Jill came to visit one of us a few years after she graduated from high school. She was enrolled in a pre-veterinarian program, and when she was talking about the classes she was taking, she described how much she disliked organic chemistry. When asked how she remained motivated to study, she commented that it was not always easy, but the fact that the course was an essential component to becoming a veterinarian motivated her to study and work hard. In other words, she understood the value the course had in helping her achieve her dream of becoming a veterinarian. As a result, she did very well in the course.

Another example comes from a district with a robust mentoring program. As a part of this program, high school students regularly visit elementary students to help them with their writing. The elementary students love working with the high schoolers, and the elementary teachers have commented that their students' writing has improved dramatically as a result. The high school students also expressed appreciation for being able to use skills and knowledge they have learned in school to support the success of younger students.

A third story comes from a district where the middle school and high school require all students to complete a capstone project (c.f. http://www.seniorproject.net/). Capstone projects are independent learning tasks where students explore a topic of their choice and present their learning to a panel of teachers and peers. In this district, students who are transitioning from middle school to high school and from high school to career or college explore topics related to courses they may take in high school or to a career they are interested in. In general, most students are very motivated to engage in these projects. While students need varying degrees of support, they often comment that these projects are some of the most valuable they engage in as students because they help them better understand what they want to do later in life.

ACTIVITY 4.2

Consider the three anecdotes discussed earlier. Each demonstrates how usefulness can leverage motivation in the classroom. However, the examples also demonstrate other facets of motivation. Create a table to make connections to other elements of motivation described in this book. We also encourage you to return to this activity as you read more.

Scenario	Connections
Jill and Organic Chemistry	
Mentoring Program	
Capstone Projects	

Social Value

Another type of value that helps students find work and learning meaningful is what Wigfield and his colleagues refer to as attainment value (Wigfield, Eccles, & Rodriguez, 1998). For the purposes of this book, we describe this as social value. In short, students perceive activities to have social value if they believe engagement in them will have a positive impact on their identities or how they are perceived by others.

Regarding promoting positive social value, next we describe a practice teachers should embrace and one they should avoid. One simple practice that can help students feel more competent and increase their perceptions of self-efficacy is guaranteeing experiences of academic success. This is discussed more fully in the next chapter, but a simple strategy for guaranteeing success is giving students time to write down thoughts and answers in response to teacher questions. We refer to these as Time-to-Write prompts. As students write down their thoughts, teachers can walk around and read what they are writing. When they see good answers from students who have a history of struggle, they can make sure to call on them so that they can experience success.

An important practice to avoid in the classroom is creating opportunities for students to compare their performance and achievement with peers (Schunk, Pintrich, & Meece, 2008). This should be avoided because it can create negative perceptions of social value. For example, in our experience, we can recall many times when tests or papers were passed back and students would compare their grades. For students who did poorly in relation to their classmates, this is a very uncomfortable and demotivating experience. For students who did well, they may feel pressured to continue high performance or may deflect acknowledgment of their achievement if appearing "smart" is undesirable in their peer group.

ACTIVITY 4.3 EXTENSION QUESTIONS

Consider these questions. Feel free to share or discuss you thoughts with colleagues.

1. What other strategies are you familiar with that could promote positive social value?

2. What are other ways schools and teachers intentionally or unintentionally undermine positive social value?

Given what we have just discussed about meaningfulness and the role value plays in designing tasks that will allow teachers to harness student motivation, it is important to keep in mind that a learning task will not seem meaningful to students just because we say it is. It is insufficient for teachers to simply tell their students how academic tasks are relevant to the world outside of school or to think that work that is meaningful and relevant to them will also be meaningful and relevant to their students. This caution emphasizes, once again, that motivation to learn is rooted in *student* perceptions of what they are supposed to be doing and learning, when and where they are doing it, with whom, and for what purpose. Thus, in short, we define meaningful learning tasks as those that are relevant to students and help students connect learning to what they value, which includes but is not limited to interests, goals, and individuals they respect or like. Next, we describe additional activities that integrate the elements of meaningful learning just described.

INTEGRATING ELEMENTS OF MEANINGFUL LEARNING INTO CLASSROOM INSTRUCTION

When designing instructional activities, teachers are encouraged to consider all the factors of meaningful learning activities discussed in this chapter. Although each element alone has the potential to guide motivation for learning, we encourage teachers to integrate as many elements as possible. High-quality instruction should be interesting; students should understand why the work is important; and ideally, activities should be constructed to encourage various ways of interacting with materials, others, and learning environments. Here we describe three strategies that illustrate how teachers can easily implement practices for making learning more meaningful.

Value-Oriented Questions

One set of strategies that can help promote perceptions of meaningfulness is for teachers to consider *who, what, when, where, why,* and *how* when designing learning tasks. These questions build on the 4WH framework described in Chapter 3 and are designed to help teachers enhance the meaningfulness of what is being learned in the classroom. When designing tasks, we encourage teachers to ask the following questions to design and frame instruction so that students see value in what they will be doing.

1. What are students doing and learning?

2. When are students expected to complete the work or stages of the work?

3. When might they need to apply this work outside of school?

4. Where are students expected to do the work?

5. Where would individuals be expected to do work like this outside of school?

6. Who will students work with?

7. Who (or what type of professionals) would need to know or be able to do this?

8. How will students engage in the work?

9. Why is the work and learning important?

Each of these questions is explored in greater depth next.

What Are Students Doing and Learning?

As mentioned in the discussion on interest earlier, students are more motivated when they are interested or will enjoy *what* they are learning in a school activity. Most teachers have seen motivation peak when students like the topic of study. In many classrooms, students and teachers have little or no control over the content and standards of what needs to be learned. Nonetheless, there are still multiple opportunities for teachers to enhance student interest in what they are learning or doing. For example, giving students choice on research topics or letting them choose from a set of readings gives them the opportunity to find the most interesting option for them. This idea is explored in more depth in Chapter 3.

It is also important to point out that the creation of Common Core State Standards for English Language Arts and Mathematics, as well as the Next Generation Science Standards, has potential to provide teachers with greater latitude for tapping into student interest. Although controversial in some respects, these standards have encouraged a shift from a content-driven curriculum to a deeper focus on application of skills and knowledge (www.achievethecore.org). Thus, rather than implement curricula that hop from topic to topic, the hope is that teachers will have greater leeway within these new standards to identify areas of higher interest within their fields and disciplines as long as they address the key concepts, skills, and processes.

Who Will We Be Working With?

Everyone cares about who they work with. Learning can become more meaningful if students get to work with peers who support their sense of relatedness or belonging (Deci & Ryan, 2002). This concept is described in greater detail in Chapter 6. Students also enjoy working with other students who they admire and can learn from. This includes respected peers or adults. For example, the mentoring program described in Activity 4.2 is so successful because it pairs elementary students with high school students they admire. Another example comes from one teacher we know who creates an opportunity every year where professional writers (e.g., local journalists, authors, web designers, etc.) come into school to conference with the students. Her students are always excited and very motivated to receive feedback from professionals who write for a living.

When and Where Will We Be Working?

Time and location matter. Often when we visit classrooms we see students working at their desks when they could be work in a variety of other locations such as the floor, at tables at the back of the room, outside, in the hallway, in the library, or in the technology center. This sounds simple but it matters to students (see Chapter 3). Similarly, it also matters when work gets done. For example, it is our experience that reading and writing tend to be assigned as homework because these activities are very time consuming. However, reading and writing are very challenging tasks. They are also two of the most important measures of academic achievement. Many teachers we have worked with have seen spikes in classroom motivation when time is devoted to reading and writing in class where the teacher can provide support as students engage in the work. Many students appreciate a teacher's willingness to create student work time. Students will be more likely to perceive value in an activity if the teacher sees enough value in it to dedicate class time supporting it.

How Will We Complete the Work?

Another factor that can make learning interesting and fun relates to Howard Gardner's (1999) work with multiple intelligences, which describe various ways individuals interact with others, their environment, and learning (see Chapter 1). In short, individuals tend to solve problems and engage with their environment in different ways. For example, some individuals understand more deeply through linguistic tasks while others learn better through kinesthetic activities. Thus, just as the content of what students are learning may be relevant, fun, or interesting; the way in which students are asked to engage with material and ideas can also be motivating when they are offered different ways to understand and demonstrate their learning.

Why Are We Learning This?

An important strategy to help students see the usefulness of what they are learning is to provide a clear rationale about what the students are doing and learning. A simple way to do this is to set the purpose early on. This helps answer some of the questions many students ask—"Why are we learning this?" or "Why are we doing this?" or "What is the point of this?" Setting the purpose early on helps to answer their questions about why. This is particularly important when we ask students to read (Fisher, Frey, & Lapp, 2009). On many occasions when we observed students reading in classrooms, we have asked students why they are reading the text at hand. The most common answer to this question is, "Because the teacher told us to." It is no surprise then that many students do not see value in what they are asked to read or why they might prefer to have the teacher tell them what they need to know rather than learn it from reading. However, we have seen that when teachers make it very clear why students are reading a particular text and what they are supposed to learn from it, students are more motivated to read. They also read more strategically.

Communicating Clear Learning Objectives

A simple, but very effective, strategy to help make learning meaningful is to communicate clear learning objectives to students (Ambrose, 2010; Moss & Brookhart, 2012). Often when we visit classrooms where teaching and learning are in progress, we quietly ask students why they are working on whatever it is they are working on. Frequently, students respond by telling us they do not know why they are doing what they are doing. In contrast, in the highly motivating classrooms we have observed, teachers make the learning objectives very clear to students. Students always know how the activities connect to important learning goals.

We provide a few guidelines to help teachers design and communicate clear learning objectives to students. First, it is important for teachers to clearly identify the learning objectives for every lesson and unit. Based on the work of a few experts in this field (e.g., Marzano, 2009; Wiggins & McTighe, 2008), we encourage teachers to make sure every learning objective includes each of the following components: the condition, the demonstration, and the criteria of performance. The condition identifies the context in which the expected learning is to take place. For example, students may be expected to demonstrate their learning after reading an article or while they are observing an experiment. The second component is the demonstration, and it focuses on clearly defining what students are expected to do. The demonstration usually asks students to show understanding of knowledge, apply specific skills or processes, or both. The demonstration is often written by stating, "Students will be able to . . . " The final component of a clearly written learning objective provides the criteria for performance. Table 4.2 provides a few examples of learning objectives that include all three components.

Once teachers have designed precise learning objectives, they must clearly communicate the objectives to students. Effective teachers often do this by writing the objectives on the board with clear, concrete, and student-friendly language. Avoid abstract language. For example, do not write an obscure objective such as *by the end of class, you will to understand plot.* Instead, try to be more specific. A middle school teacher could write, *By the end of class you will be able to describe the setting, trigger, conflict, and resolution in the short story "The Most Dangerous Game."* An elementary teacher might write, *By the end of the story, you will be able to explain why the main character in the story, Pinkalicious, turns pink.*

Referencing the Objectives

The third suggestion for communicating clear learning objectives is to refer to the objective *multiple times* throughout a lesson. For example, in a recent high school science classroom, as students read the biology textbook, the teacher kept telling them, "Remember, your task is to be able to define photosynthesis and explain how it works by the end of the class. Focus on that as you read!" In short, when students know why they are learning something and how activities connect to larger learning goals, they are more likely to see why the work is relevant.

Table 4.1   Writing Clear Learning Targets

Objective Statement	Condition	Demonstration	Criteria
After watching and discussing a video on how diseases are transmitted, students will be able to independently list and describe at least two common ways the flu can be spread and three essential steps individuals can take to limit exposure.	After watching and discussing a video on how diseases are transmitted,	students will be able to independently list and describe at least two common ways the flu can be spread and three essential steps individuals can take to limit exposure.	List and describe **independently** . . . list and describe **two** common ways **three** essential steps
After being given a word problem, students will be able to independently represent the word problem by translating the problem into variables and symbols.	After being given a word problem,	students will be able to represent the word problem	by **independently** translating the problem into variables.
While reading the short story *The Most Dangerous Game*, students will be able to determine the moves the author makes to build suspense by working in cooperative groups to underline and label instances where suspense is increased.	While reading the short story *The Most Dangerous Game*,	students will be able to determine the moves the author makes to build suspense	by working in cooperative groups to underline and label instances where suspense is increased.

Relevance Mapping

A strategy that we developed to help students understand the meaningfulness of a learning activity is relevance mapping. Sometimes when students want to know why they are engaging in a specific activity it helps to have them map out its relevance or importance. The teacher in the River View Middle School case study, Mr. Gardner, frequently asked the students to do *quick writes* (Buehl, 2001) before answering questions. When a couple of students wanted to know why Mr. Gardner was always having them jot down their thoughts he asked them to brainstorm situations in which they could envision it being useful to record their thoughts before acting. Figure 4.2 illustrates some of what the students generated.

After the students mapped out their thoughts on the whiteboard, Mr. White asked the students to respond to the following prompt: *How might the practice of quick writes be useful or relevant to you after high school?* After the students completed their responses, Mr. White was amazed by what the students wrote. All but one of the students was able to see quick writes in a new light. They realized that quick writes were not just another type of busy work that Mr. White was giving them. They saw that the habit of writing down thoughts before speaking or acting helped them process and organize their ideas. Some students realized that it helped them think more deeply and to be more thoughtful. As one student left the class, she told Mr. White that she never realized such a simple skill could be so useful.

Chapter Summary

Building on the last chapter on promoting student voice, this chapter focused on the importance of making learning meaningful and helping students find meaningfulness in what they are doing. To connect back to our guiding metaphor of rafting, people could have different reasons for engaging in this activity. In other words, they could *want* to do it for various reasons. Paddlers could engage in the task because they are interested in it and find the activity enjoyable. Others could

Figure 4.2   Sample Relevance Map

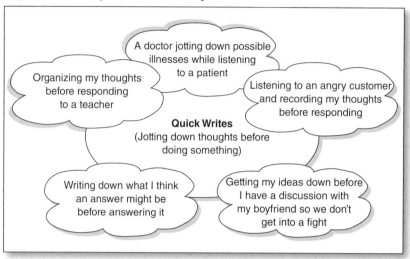

perceive meaning elsewhere. For example, we have heard of many groups using rafting as an activity to help coworkers develop effective communication skills. On the other hand, an activity such as rafting could also have high social value because it is an opportunity for participants to get to know one another better. Regardless of the reasons, what does not change is the importance of clearly helping students understand and perceive the value in whatever it is they are doing.

At this point, we encourage readers to reconsider and discuss the River View scenario at the beginning of this chapter. Why do you think students find this project so meaningful? When we share this example with teachers, many do not believe it is real. It is. Some have questioned the practicality of such a project. We recognize that such an experience sets a high bar and clearly could not be repeated in other contexts. But is serves as a creative example of a project developed by teachers who successfully sought and tapped into a local community resource to construct a meaningful learning experience for students. We hope some of the examples in this book will encourage readers to identify similar opportunities and develop meaningful experiences that have potential in their local contexts and communities.

CHAPTER WRAP-UP ACTIVITY

Planning for and integrating components of meaningfulness into learning activities requires critical reflection. The Meaningfulness Survey at the end of this chapter is designed to help teachers determine the extent to which instructional tasks in the classroom are meaningful to students. This tool can be used in a variety of ways. Teachers are encouraged to complete it on their own to determine areas of relative strength and weaknesses. We also encourage teachers to give the survey to students. Because, ultimately, students determine the meaningfulness of tasks, the survey also provides valuable data about how students perceive tasks and activities.

Directions

1. In the space provided on the following page, briefly describe a project, unit, or activity that you have recently used with students. Consider using an activity that did not go as well as planned. Or select a project that is representative of the type of activities you use with your students on a regular basis.

2. After you have described the activity, consider and respond to each reflection question in the space provided.

3. After responding to each question, explain the reasoning for you answer.

4. Considering giving the student survey to students with the activity section filled out.

5. After collecting the student responses, compare their responses to yours.

6. Once you (and the students) have completed the sheet, consider what changes you might make to enhance the meaningfulness of the activity. You may also share data from these sheets with colleagues to brainstorm strategies for increasing meaningfulness.

Meaningfulness Survey (Teacher Version)

Activity or Project Description:

Reflection Questions	Yes	No	Rationale
Did the lesson, activity, or project have high interest value?	☐	☐	
Was the activity, lesson, or project useful to students?	☐	☐	
Did the lesson, activity, or project have high social value?	☐	☐	
Did the students clearly understand the objective or purpose?	☐	☐	
Why are students doing the work and learning what they will be learning?	☐	☐	
How will students be engaging in the work?	☐	☐	

What adjustments would make the activity or project more meaningful?

Meaningfulness Survey (Student Version)

Activity or Project Description:

Reflection Questions	Yes	No	Why or Why Not
Was the activity, lesson, or project interesting?	☐	☐	
Was the activity, lesson, or project useful or helpful?	☐	☐	
Did you like the activity, lesson, or project?	☐	☐	
Do you know what were you supposed to learn?	☐	☐	
Did you learn it?	☐	☐	

What ideas to you have to make the activity, lesson, or project better?

5

Promoting Challenge With Success

A classroom aide nudged Rashad, "Do you have your work today?"

Rashad replied sheepishly, "Um... yeah... somewhere." He produced a piece of paper with only a few answers on it. It looked like something he had done quickly on the bus just to get it done. The aide recalled a team meeting with Rashad's parents earlier in the year in which they explained his history with math. "Ever since second grade, he has struggled with math," she remembered Rashad's mother reporting. "At home he can do the math problems if I sit with him, but he freezes up when he works on them alone. Mostly he just tries to avoid math all together."

CASE STUDY ANALYSIS QUESTION SET 5.1

1. Why do you think Rashad tries to avoid doing math?

2. How do you think Rashad would describe his level of competence in math?

3. How do you think Rashad would feel about math if he had had greater success with math in elementary school?

4. What are some teaching activities or topics you avoid more than others?

5. How would you describe your level of competence in the teaching activities you avoid?

6. How would you describe your history with the content and skills related to the activities you tend to avoid more than others?

THE ROLES OF SUCCESS AND CHALLENGE

Students will be motivated when they have success or believe they will be successful on tasks that have an appropriate or optimal level of challenge (Csikszentmihalyi, 2005; Turner et al., 1995). For our purposes here, we define success in school as the demonstration of mastery, competence, or adequate progress on specific learning tasks. **Challenge** refers to the extent to which a learning task is well matched to a student's current knowledge or skills with the purpose of improving or increasing them. For challenge with success to strengthen motivation to learn, students must perceive both of the following: that the task is challenging in meaningful and appropriate ways (see Chapter 4) and that they can be successful with it. Next, we explore important factors teachers should consider when supporting students to be successful on challenging tasks.

DESIGNING APPROPRIATE CHALLENGE

When students experience success on challenging tasks, their motivation to engage in similarly challenging tasks is likely to increase. The reason for this is that success with difficult assignments can increase a students' perception of their competence and, in turn, increase feelings of self-efficacy when faced with similar tasks (Moneta & Csikszentmihalyi, 1996).

However, the appropriate or optimal level of challenge for each student on any given task is difficult to determine because it is influenced by each student's belief about the probability of success. Students' perceptions of their competence and their feelings of self-efficacy play a key role in determining how much effort to apply, how hard to persevere through challenges, and how resilient they will be in the face of adversity (Schunk & Pajares, 2005). For example, in the River View Middle School scenario in Chapter 1, compare Jennifer's and Rashad's reactions to the math problems.

Students' perception of competence often develops from prior experiences. Therefore, when designing tasks, it is essential for teachers to consider each student's history of success and failure with the skills and concepts related to the activities involved. Students who have histories of being more successful will likely have high levels of self-efficacy and will be likely able to tolerate high levels of challenge. On the other hand, students who have histories of struggle or failure may have very little self-efficacy and little or no tolerance for challenge (Miller, 2003). Students with lower self-efficacy will benefit from engaging in tasks with little challenge to build and strengthen their sense of competence. For example, consider young children who are learning to read. They will often read the same book over and over again. Young children do this because they are developing self-efficacy as readers. Each time a child rereads a book successfully, it reinforces her emerging awareness that she can read. As perceptions of competence increase, students become more ready and willing to read newer and harder material.

Given that the challenge level of any single task will be perceived differently by multiple students, it is extremely difficult for teachers to know how to support students without getting input from the students themselves. There are a variety of strategies that allow teachers to determine how students are evaluating the complexity of a task and if they find a task too easy or too difficult. Preassessments give teachers useful information about how much students know or can do before engaging in a lesson or unit. Student self-assessments of their knowledge and skills as well as about the perceived challenge of a task are also extremely valuable. Examples of each are provided at the end of this chapter.

Based on what teachers learn from and know about their students, in general, we encourage teachers to apply what we call the Goldilocks Principle when designing instructional tasks. This is also referred to as "optimal challenge (Guay, Ratelle, & Chanal, 2008; Turner et al., 1996). This principle encourages teachers to design tasks that are not too hard and not too easy. To do this, it is useful to consider features of tasks that influence students' perception of challenge. Characteristics that make a task appear too challenging often include a perceived lack of the following: clarity around procedures and outcomes, knowledge and skills needed to complete the task, and related experience. In addition to these features, a history of failure around the knowledge, skills, or experiences related to the task will exacerbate a student's perception of the difficulty of that task and increase the likelihood of avoidance behaviors. On the other hand, features that make a task appear too easy or not challenging enough include a lack of novelty, as well as appearing too simple or not complex enough.

Scaffolding for Success

As mentioned earlier, students' beliefs about their competence and their expectations about the likelihood of success on challenging tasks also play an important role in determining the extent to which they will be motivated to engage in any classroom activity. Their beliefs influence how long they will persevere when challenge increases (Wigfield & Eccles, 2002). A variety of factors influence students' perceptions about their potential success. Some factors include the following: (a) clarity of what success looks like, (b) how students perceive their own competence, (c) a fixed or growth mindset, (d) students' history with success and failure, (e) comfort in the context where the activity will take place, as well as (f) the amount of support that will be provided. We describe each of these factors in more depth next.

Being clear about what success looks like. When designing instructional activities, it is essential to clearly define what success will look like (Marzano, 2003). For example, in the scenario that opened this chapter, it is very likely that Rashad did not have a clear understanding of what success looks like for him in math. Considering his struggle in mathematics, he may feel that the mathematical learning he is doing in school is a never-ending battle. Too often students do not have a clear understanding of the objectives of a learning task. As a result, this lack of clarity makes it very difficult for students to understand what success looks like. Without clarity, students will not know what to do to be successful. As teachers, we need to make sure to clearly explain and show how the objectives of lessons are being applied, provide examples of successful work, and describe the features or characteristics of successful work. On longer projects, it is important to also break the tasks into clear milestones or benchmarks so that students can see their progress.

Emphasize competence. Another factor to consider when supporting students' success on tasks is each student's perception of personal competence. Perceptions of competence are often based on an individual's history of success or failure on a specific task or with skills related to the task (Deci & Ryan, 2002). Therefore, teachers must help students break cycles of failure. For example, in the scenario earlier, Rashad clearly has a history of failure and struggle with math. When students have such a history, they tend to avoid engaging in a task. The longer or deeper the history of failure, the more a student will work to avoid the activity altogether (Turner et al., 2002). Therefore, it is important for teachers to learn about and consider each student's history with variables related to the work they are being asked to do. When students have histories of failure or experienced lack of success, which may be as recent as the previous learning task, it is important to support students by taking a variety of steps to insure success and increase feelings of competence.

Encouraging a growth mindset. In her popular book, *Mindset: The New Psychology of Success,* Dweck (2008) discusses the importance of emphasizing and praising students' effort, not their abilities. To understand the difference between praising ability (e.g., "Wow! You are really talented!) versus praising effort (e.g., "I am impressed with how much effort you put into your practicing. It really paid off!"), Dweck describes two different mindsets that influence how individuals approach challenging tasks. An individual with a *fixed mindset* approaches a task thinking that his abilities will define success and that these abilities tend to be set in stone or fixed in place. A fixed mindset typically believes that many challenging tasks are an all or nothing endeavor. A person will either fail or succeed. On the other hand, a person with a *growth mindset* believes that her abilities are malleable and can improve through perseverance and hard work. For individuals with a growth mindset, challenging tasks are an opportunity for growth and improvement.

The ways we praise and encourage students can influence the type of mindset students will apply when tackling challenging tasks. Praise that emphasizes talent and abilities promotes a fixed mindset. Such a mindset is often intolerant to failure. This is especially true for advanced students. For example, many of us can recall times where advanced students who were used to getting straight A's struggle or shut down when the difficulty of a task challenges their current level of ability. This is often because some students who excel attribute their success to their abilities. When they fail, they view that failure as an indication that their belief in their abilities was not accurate.

When we praise students' effort, we should strive to emphasize a growth mindset. This reinforces the suggestion that hard work and perseverance produce success. A growth mindset also views failure as a learning opportunity that promotes improvement, and does not view challenging tasks as a zero sum game. Thus, when we praise students for their effort, we promote a spirit of perseverance and grit that goes a long way to supporting success when engaging in challenging tasks.

Provide consistent support. Finally, students' perceptions about the amount or level of support for an activity or task will also shape their motivation to learn (McCombs, 2010). This is increasingly important as the challenge level of a task increases or when challenge is not optimal. If students understand how they will be supported as well as how this support will increase their chances of success, they will more likely engage in the task in a motivated manner (Reddy, Rhodes, & Mulhall, 2003). Thus, teachers can make it clear how they will support students by explaining what supports are available if students need help as well as when and how they should request the support.

BALANCING CHALLENGE AND SUCCESS

When it comes to harnessing motivation in the classroom, success and challenge go hand-in-hand. In other words, challenge without success is often demotivating; on the other hand, success without challenge, in many instances, is meaningless. However, there is an important caveat here. As mentioned earlier, students with histories of failure need to build a history of success before engaging in challenging tasks. This means, not all activities require optimal challenge. In addition, there are instances when students need to practice skills to build fluency or automaticity (e.g., mastering the times tables), focus on process rather than product, or produce something for expert evaluation (e.g., showcase).

Finding the optimal balance of challenge and success is difficult. One area where this idea of optimal challenge can inform teaching is gaming. Gee (2003) in *What Video Games Have to Teach Us About Learning and Literacy* shows us that video-game makers are masters of balancing challenge and success to motivate gamers. Gee describes how video games are strategically designed to compel individuals to keep playing and explores how these methods can be used in classrooms. Three important things that video games do are the following. First, they provide useful and often instantaneous *feedback* about performance. Second, they provide multiple opportunities for gamers (learners) to apply the information gained from the feedback to make adjustments and *self-regulate* their decisions during the activity. Third, video games *gradually* increase challenge as players continue to gain and use feedback to improve their play on a continual basis. Next, we discuss the importance of feedback, self-regulation, and gradual increase of challenge in greater detail.

ENGAGING IN FORMATIVE ASSESSMENT PRACTICES

Over the past few years, we have seen a rising interest in formative assessment at the classroom level. Many educators view formative assessment as small tests or tasks that are given more frequently than traditional tests or quizzes. However, Margaret Heritage (2013) points out that formative assessment should be a daily *practice.* She argues that the purpose of formative assessment is to "move students' learning forward while their learning is still in the process of developing" (p. 18). Thus, teachers should be monitoring students' learning on an ongoing basis and providing them with feedback continuously.

PROVIDING TIMELY AND USEFUL FEEDBACK

Feedback is arguably the most important ingredient for effective teaching and learning (Hattie, 2009). Feedback is also an essential element of formative assessment practice and progress monitoring. Pollock (2012) defines feedback as "assessment of progress toward a goal." As such, feedback must not only include useful information to determine how well one is progressing toward a goal, but also it must also be timely. Useful information can come from a variety of sources (e.g., from a teacher, a student's peers, or from data collected by the students themselves). It can also take a variety of forms (e.g., quantitative or qualitative). However, in many instances, useful feedback should include the following: (a) positive information about progress toward specific goals, (b) information about challenges or obstacles that are impeding or potentially impeding progress, and (c) information about strategies or approaches to continue forward progress and overcome any challenges.

MORE STRATEGIES FOR BALANCING CHALLENGE AND SUCCESS

In Chapter 4, we discussed the importance of clearly communicating learning targets to students. It is just as important for students to understand *what* they will be doing to meet learning targets. If students do not understand what they will be doing with extreme clarity, they may think the tasks are too easy or too hard. Next are four areas of instructional strategies that are designed to make clear to students what they are being asked to do and how challenging it will be.

Clear Directions

Writing and stating clear directions is almost an art form. In our experience, most teachers acknowledge that they have written directions or given oral directions that unintentionally confused students at times. We have done this ourselves. While all teachers make mistakes, it is helpful to have strategic guidelines to follow to improve the chances that our directions will be clear to students. The following are some rules to follow when writing directions or instructions for students.

1. Provide an informative title (e.g., "How to Edit a Peer's Essay" or "How to Edit a Photograph Using iPhoto").

2. Keep it simple. Use short sentences. Do not include multiple actions in a single sentence.

3. Use verbs at the beginning of sentences that describe what you want students to do.

4. Use visual cues, such as bullets or diagrams, if many steps are involved.

5. Write steps in a logical order.

6. Keep the directions or instructions short. If they lengthy, consider dividing them into sections or parts, each with its own header.

7. Request feedback from a few students on an early draft of the instructions or directions.

The rules are helpful for a variety of reasons. First, when directions are clear, students have a better understanding of the task. If a task is unclear, students may not be able to find the meaningfulness in it (see Chapter 4). Regarding challenge and success, obscure directions undermine students' perceptions of self-efficacy. If they do not understand what a task or activity is asking from them, they will likely doubt their ability to engage in or complete it successfully.

Preassessments

Preassessments are a powerful, but underused strategy in classrooms (Marzano, 2006). Think about your own practices. How often do you preassess student learning? If this is something you typically do, great. Then consider how your preassessments might impact student perceptions of challenge and their possible success. In short, preassessments are the same assessment or are a very similar assessment that students will take at the end of a unit, project, lesson, or series of lessons. Preassessments work best when the assessment is practical and not extremely time consuming. For example, if students are taking a traditional pencil-paper assessment at the end of a unit or series of lessons, give them a similar, but more abbreviated assessment before you begin instruction. A simple strategy that can be used at any level is something we call Three-Minute Writing. With this strategy, give students three minutes to write down everything they know about a topic.

The information students provide during this activity provides teachers with information about what students know and do not know. Teachers can use this information to make important adjustments to their instruction.

Knowledge Rating Charts

Another preassessment strategy that teachers can use to preassess students' knowledge of essential terms and vocabulary is a Knowledge Rating Chart (Meltzer & Jackson, 2010). To use this strategy, teachers create a chart similar to the sample displayed in Table 5.1. Give the chart to students. They can work alone, in pairs, or small groups. For each word in the table, students identify if they (1) know the word well, (2) have seen it or heard it, or (3) have no clue what it means. If students check off that they know the word well or are somewhat familiar with it, they must then record what the word means or what they think it means. This is an excellent activity to determine how much knowledge students have about key terms and if there are some words that need more or less support from the teacher.

Some teachers may worry that giving an assessment at the beginning undermines the learning. Some teachers claim that preassessment feels like cheating (i.e., showing the test in advance). For example, a middle school science teacher may want students to know the main parts to a plant cell. Her assessment might include a diagram or illustration that asks students to label the parts of a cell. One might worry

Table 5.1 Sample Knowledge Rating Chart

Terms	Know It Well	Seen It / Heard It	No Clue	Definition
Photosynthesis				
Energy				
Respiration				

that giving this diagram before students have engaged in any lessons, defeats the purpose. It does not. It does do two things, however. First, it makes it very clear to students what they need to learn and how their learning will be assessed. Second, it shows the teacher and each student what he or she does know and does not know. This is extremely important. If some students know most of the cell parts, then the teacher will know this early on and be able to adjust learning activities to meet the needs of these students. If the teacher were not to do this, there is a good chance these students would have been bored (i.e., not optimally challenged). On the other hand, if students realize they do not know most if not all of the cell parts, then there is a good chance they will be challenged during the learning activities.

Models and Exemplars

Some projects and activities are too large or time consuming to use as a preassessment. When this is the case, it is very helpful to give students examples of high-quality work—the type of work that the teacher wants the students to be able to produce. Oftentimes, when we recommend this strategy, teachers comment that they might be doing an activity for the first time and do not have any examples of proficient or exemplary student work. This is not a problem. Rather than use actual student work, teachers can do their own project or find examples on the Internet. There are at least two benefits to doing this. First, the teacher has control to make sure the work demonstrates the defining features of the project, and they can use the model or exemplars to emphasize these important components. Second, when teachers actually do the work they will be asking students to complete, they have a much better understanding of task or tasks involved. When we do this with our own teaching, we often see details, steps, or elements of the work that we initially missed.

Giving students models or samples of the type of work they are being asked to reproduce makes it very clear to students what the teacher is asking them to do. Thus, at the very beginning students will have a sense of whether the work will be too easy or too hard. Therefore, it is important when sharing sample work with students to ask them how confident they feel in being able to do the work. If they are overly worried, the teacher can work with the students to determine what additional supports would improve confidence.

Demonstrations and Think-Alouds

In addition to giving students a model or exemplar of finished work when a process is somewhat complicated, it is very helpful to give the students a demonstration. Different types of modeling can be done in a variety of simple and creative ways. For example, math teachers frequently demonstrate how to solve problems by providing a generic format and then demonstrating how to use it (e.g., the lattice method, the Pythagorean theorem). Elementary teachers commonly show students what they will be doing by acting out the task or illustrating how to complete it using a document camera (e.g., measuring with a ruler, identifying vowels). One ingenious teacher we know created a display of the writing process for a literary essay. She engaged in the process herself and displayed her work at every stage of the process—from her initial notes and freewriting to the initial rough drafts to the final, edited draft.

Sometimes the academic work we ask students to do is cognitive and invisible. When this is the case, think-alouds (Olson, Duffy, & Mack, 1984) are a very useful strategy to "show" students what the learning activity will require them to do in their heads. For example, when using a think-aloud, a math teacher might demonstrate how to solve a problem, and while doing the problem, she would "think out loud" to demonstrate the questions she was asking and the decisions she was making. She can even talk about the mistakes she made and how she verified her answer. A teacher might think out loud to show students how to ask questions when they are reading a text or how to find information by using the text headings and graphs and charts.

Models and exemplars also go hand-in-hand with rubrics. In our experience, we have found that many teachers create and use rubrics to help students understand how they will be assessed. We believe that rubrics are sometimes difficult for students to comprehend. However, when a rubric is accompanied by examples or models, the exemplars illustrate what the rubric is describing. One powerful practice that we have seen in many classrooms is where teachers use models to coconstruct a rubric with students. When students help develop the rubrics that will be used to assess their learning, they are more likely to understand what success looks like and use this information to guide their learning. Such an approach also works to promote student voice in the classroom (see Chapter 3).

CHAPTER SUMMARY

In the previous two chapters, we explored the roles of student voice and meaningfulness in leveraging student motivation in the classroom. This chapter introduced another pair of concepts—challenge with success. As mentioned earlier, promoting student voice and creating meaningful activities by themselves are often not enough to design activities that will result in high levels of motivation and engagement. It is also essential for teachers to do their best to match each student with an optimal level of challenge as it relates to their knowledge, skills, and past experiences. It is also important to point out that when we give students voice in determining the challenge level of activities, they often do a better job than us in finding the right level of challenge. A clear example of this comes from a third grade teacher we know. A few weeks after school begins in the fall, this teacher provides students with a weekly spelling list. In addition to the standard list, the students are also asked to select additional words from books they are reading to add to the list. This teacher is always amazed at the difficulty level of the words most of the students select. She also found that the students are very motivated to learn how to spell these words. This should come as no surprise at this point. With this simple strategy, the teacher has promoted student voice, helped the students find meaning in the words on their spelling list (they are words they selected and *want* to know how to spell), and the words tend to be very challenging. Last, while many of the words are challenging, the students do pick words they think they will be able to learn. In most cases they are successful.

CHAPTER WRAP-UP ACTIVITY

The self-assessment on the following page is designed to help teachers determine the extent to which instructional tasks in the classroom are appropriately challenging and scaffolded for success. This tool can be used in a variety of ways. Teachers are encouraged to complete the tool on their own to determine areas of relative strength and weaknesses. We also encourage teachers to give similar questions to the students after lessons and activities have been completed. After the self-assessment, we also provide a sample student questionnaire that can be used in many contexts. Once teachers have completed the self-assessment and/or collected data from the students, they can identify areas where they work to provide a better match of challenge and success.

SELF-ASSESSMENT FOR CHALLENGE WITH SUCCESS

Making Objectives and Tasks Clear

In general, how frequently do students understand **what** they have to do and **why**?

Routinely	Frequently	Occasionally	Rarely	Never
1	2	3	4	5

Describe strategies that are used to make objectives and tasks clear.

What could be done to make objectives and tasks more clear?

Providing Appropriate Levels of Challenge

How frequently is the difficultly level of tasks "**just right?**"

Routinely	Frequently	Occasionally	Rarely	Never
1	2	3	4	5

How often are tasks **too hard**?

Routinely	Frequently	Occasionally	Rarely	Never
1	2	3	4	5

How often are tasks **too easy**?

Routinely	Frequently	Occasionally	Rarely	Never
1	2	3	4	5

Describe strategies that are used to make sure that tasks are the right level of challenge for each student.

What could be done to improve the challenge level of lessons, tasks, and activities?

Giving Immediate and Informative Feedback

How frequently do students receive **immediate** feedback when working on or after work on a lesson or task?

Routinely	Frequently	Occasionally	Rarely	Never
1	2	3	4	5

How frequently do students receive **informative** feedback when working on or after work on a lesson or task?

Routinely	Frequently	Occasionally	Rarely	Never
1	2	3	4	5

Describe strategies that are used to give students quick and useful feedback about their learning and work.

What could be done to improve the timeliness and usefulness of feedback?

STUDENT QUESTIONNAIRE

Directions

Please take a few minutes to consider the lesson or activity we just completed and to honestly respond to each of the questions.

1. What was the purpose of the lesson or activity?

2. Was the lesson or activity too easy, too hard, or just right? Why?

3. Were you successful? Why or why not?

4. What helped you learn the most?

5. What got in the way of you learning?

ADDTIONAL FEEDBACK

6

Building Positive Relationships Around Learning

After lunch, Jennifer and Rashad were on their way to health class. Rashad was talking excitedly about a project they were working on in class and Jennifer was listening intently.

"And then Mrs. Zales let me and Max try out one of our ideas in the back while the rest of the students continued working on their experiments and lab reports!"

Jennifer smiled at Rashad. "Wow. You really like science! My class is just so boring."

Rashad paused for a moment. "You know—I am not so sure it is just because of the science stuff. Mrs. Zales really cares about us. She really pushes us to work hard and challenges us, but she also understands when we make mistakes. I also like a lot of the activities she puts together. When we work in groups—the time flies. We just really work well together in that class!"

"That's cool," replied Jennifer. "I wish my science class was more like that! My science teacher doesn't really seem to care all that much about us. He even calls me by the wrong name sometimes."

CASE STUDY ANALYSIS QUESTION SET 6.1

1. Based on the short excerpt, why do you think Rashad feels a strong connection to the teacher and students in his class?

2. Why do you think Jennifer might not feel the same way about hers?

3. How do you demonstrate to students that you care about them?

4. How do you encourage students to demonstrate caring attitudes toward one another?

5. What are some specific examples of actions you have done recently that demonstrate caring to the students?

RELATIONSHIPS MATTER FOR MOTIVATION

Relationships matter—they matter at home, at play, and at work. A variety of research supports what we fundamentally know about the importance positive relationships play in our lives, particularly the influence they can have on motivation and achievement. Deci and Ryan (2002) described feelings of relatedness as one of the three pillars of intrinsic motivation. They define relatedness as the need to feel connected to others, to care for and be cared for by others, and to feel as if one belongs with other individuals and as a part of one's communities (p. 7). As Deci and Ryan explain throughout their research, to feel motivated, individuals need to perceive a sense of autonomy, competence, and relatedness. Therefore, while we may encourage student voice to promote feelings of autonomy (Chapter 4), and while we may challenge students and scaffold for individual success to build a sense of competence (Chapter 5), doing so is often more effective when the learning in which we attempt to engage students happens in partnership with others through positive relationships grounded in authentic caring.

A key element in building positive relationships in classrooms is the relationship teachers have with students. One growing body of research suggests that when teachers display caring attitudes toward students—what is often called "an ethic of care"—a variety of positive outcomes occur (Noddings, 2005; 2006). Some of these outcomes include, but are not limited to, increased motivation to learn, greater perseverance during challenging work, increased attendance, lower dropout rates, and overall improvements in academic achievement (Cornelius-White & Harbaugh, 2010; Grant & Sleeter, 2007; Hebert & Durham, 2008; Wilson, 2006).

Not only are positive relationships with teachers important, it is also essential to encourage students to develop and sustain positive relationships with their peers (Anderman & Anderman, 2010). Again, a variety of positive outcomes have been associated with healthy peer relations including successful transitions between elementary, middle, and high school (Juvonen & Wentzel, 1996), decreases in risky behaviors (Card, Giuliano, & National Bureau of Economic Research 2011; Clark & Lohéac, 2005), increased academic motivation (Pajares & Urdan, 2002; Cotterell, 2007), and academic achievement (Francis, Skelton, & Read, 2012). In addition, positive relationships with teachers and other students together help foster a sense of belonging in school and within the classroom, which is also associated with outcomes similar to those described earlier (Bagnall & Cassity, 2012; Erwin, 2004; Halaby, 2000).

For the purposes of this book, we define positive relationships that help leverage motivation to learn as those in which teachers demonstrate caring for all students and encourage students to demonstrate caring for others through the learning in their classroom. What follows are research-based practices and strategies to help teachers create and sustain positive relations with and among students. The first set of strategies focus on the teacher-student relationship. The second group of strategies is designed to support the development of positive peer interactions.

STRATEGIES AND APPROACHES FOR POSITIVE STUDENT-TEACHER RELATIONSHIPS

The strategies in this section, as well as many described throughout the book, can help teachers develop positive relationships with students. Readers may have noticed by now that most of the strategies described in this book support multiple facets of motivation, particularly the importance of helping students develop strong and positive relationships with their teachers and peers. Many, if not all, of the strategies already described help build effective teacher-student relationships. For example, supporting student voice and decision making helps students feel valued and promotes a perception that the teacher cares (Chapter 4).

An important point that we want to emphasize is that teachers should work to build positive relationships by (1) establishing a learning environment that is caring, safe, and encourages students to take intellectual risks and (2) designing learning activities that encourage students to form positive relationships *through* the work and not apart from it. Some of the common mistakes we see teachers make in classrooms are to design activities that are fun or interesting but irrelevant to the learning that needs to take place or to *only* form relationships with students regarding their interests and achievements outside of the classroom (e.g., on sports teams, as student leaders).

Little Things Mean a Lot

It may sound simplistic and obvious, but one of the biggest things teachers can do to foster a strong and positive relationship is to take the time to do little things for a student, even things that might go unnoticed by most of the other students (Mendler, 2000). This could mean recommending or bringing in a book a student might enjoy related to the class topic; working with a student during lunch or after school to support their success or interest in learning more; sending a quick e-mail, leaving a voicemail, or sending a postcard of praise or support to the student. Making sure the parents are recipients as well is also effective. This is particularly important to do for students who are struggling or who appear to be chronically disengaged.

Mendler (2000) describes a simple strategy that he calls the Two-Minute Intervention. This strategy is designed to strengthen the relationship with a student who frequently appears unmotivated. This strategy calls for a teacher devoting two minutes a day for 10 consecutive days. During this time, the teacher initiates and engages the student in a positive interaction about anything that might be of interest to the student. Mendler emphasizes that this is not a time to bring up poor achievement or low motivation. He writes that this "is a time when you can get to know the student and the student can get to know you, without either being encumbered by expectations. Initially, the educator and the students may experience reluctance and awkwardness. It is for this reason, as well as to establish a pattern of reaching out, that the ten consecutive days is the goal" (p. 52). As this simple strategy describes, a sustained pattern of showing interest in students can do much to harness student motivation.

ACTIVITY 6.1

To develop some ideas about little things that might be meaningful to your students, begin by making a list of five to ten students you are most worried about. Consider what you know about each of them. Then think about something you could do—something small—that would be appreciated by them and would support them in the work and learning they need to do. Begin with this.

Keep Your Word

Once again, this may sound obvious, but another important strategy for building strong positive relationships with teachers is to make sure you keep your word. This is an essential component to developing a culture of caring in the classroom (Noddings, 2005; 2006). From our work in schools, we have observed teachers who are well-intentioned and usually mean what they say. However, following through with all of our good intentions is not always so easy—especially when, as teachers, we wear so many hats and juggle so many responsibilities at once. For example, during the year, a teacher may tell a student that he will try to make one of his baseball games, but never does. Or a teacher may say she will put the homework on the website or save it in a folder to be available when students are absent. In short, make sure when you say you will do something to do your best to follow through. If, as will sometimes happen, you are not able to meet your best of intentions, acknowledge this and apologize to the student or students involved.

Put It In Writing

One of the biggest questions we get from teachers is how to effectively harness motivation in a class with significant behavior management issues. While this book does not focus on behavior management per se, we do believe that classrooms and learning environments with high levels of motivation have significantly fewer behavioral issues. Conversely, students who also have significant behavior issues also tend to form low-quality relationships with teachers and peers (Pianta & Steinberg, 1992; Hamre & Pianta, 2006). That being said, there are times when students struggle to follow the rules and when they need help meeting their expectations and responsibilities. We firmly believe that when this happens it is an opportunity for growth and an opportunity to strengthen the student-teacher relationship.

One strategy we have used in the classroom and have seen used effectively by many others are individual student contracts (Marzano & Marzano, 2003). For example, at one point in his career, Kevin taught in a self-contained classroom with 18 fifth and sixth grade students in a school that primarily serves students with special needs. All of the 18 students were dyslexic, most had been diagnosed with ADHD, one had Tourette syndrome, another had Asperger syndrome, and another had been diagnosed with obsessive compulsive disorder. One might think that this classroom was fated to be frequently disruptive and unruly. On the contrary, it was one of the most, if not the most, motivated (and energetic) classrooms Kevin has had the pleasure to teach in. One of the most effective strategies he used to build strong relationships with students was individual contracts.

In short, contracts are an agreement between the student and teacher. Usually the point of the contract is to produce a particular outcome and to clearly define the student's and teacher's responsibilities and actions. Contract writing need not be a highly formal endeavor, but it is often best to put the terms of the contract in writing. At times, it is also helpful to have a timeline and a reward. Contracts also work best when they are developed jointly between the teacher and the student. The teacher should make the purpose and the intended outcomes of the contract clear to the student. In addition, the student should be given voice in the details of the contract so that he or she will find it meaningful and see value in it. For example, on one occasion a student in Kevin's classroom was having difficulty refraining from calling out whenever a teacher asked a question. The student was having difficulty controlling this impulse, but did not like it when the teacher would point it our every time it happened. Therefore, Kevin and the student met and developed a contract. The contract described a code that only Kevin and the student would understand. Whenever the student would call out, Kevin would scratch the back of his head to remind the student what he was doing (this was the student's idea). Both Kevin and student agreed that every few times the student did not call out, Kevin would call on him first. This simple plan made a world of difference. It gave the student the opportunity to learn how to self-regulate his behavior without feeling embarrassed. In fact, the student asked Kevin to share the plan with other teachers because he found it so helpful. In sum, sitting down to develop the contract allowed a frustrating situation to become an opportunity to strengthen the student-teacher relationship and support the student's learning.

There are a few additional points about contracts that are important to consider. First, be judicious in their use and make sure they are meaningful. Too many contracts are unwieldy and make it difficult for teachers to follow through with their responsibilities. Another important consideration is to keep contracts focused on the individual and to be discrete. Many students do not like others to sense that they are being singled out. However, when teachers make it clear they care and personalize the contract to a student's needs with discretion, the result can be quite powerful and lasting.

Make Learning Visible

In a recent synthesis of metaanalyses on achievement, Hattie (2009) concluded that one of the simplest ways to increase achievement in the classroom is to make learning visible. In short, learning becomes visible when we clearly understand what we need to learn and why; when we are able to monitor our progress; and ultimately, when we see that we have learned or grown. We also believe it is a powerful way to build motivation and strengthen positive student-teacher relationships, primarily because the teacher often has the capacity to make learning visible. There are many ways a teacher can make learning visible to students. Some ways are comparing student work to models, charting progress, and demonstrating growth.

A powerful way to make a student's learning visible is to display the students' work back to them. There are numerous ways to do this. One of our favorites is to use video. For example, one teacher we know used a smart phone to capture video of students' presentations. After the students had pre-sented the first time, he met with the students individually. He showed them a recording of a high-quality presentation first. In this case, the teacher had recorded himself giving a presentation like the one he wanted students to provide (mod-eling and demonstration, Chapter 5). Then he showed each student's presentation and asked that student to identify two or three areas for improvement. Once they had done that, they made a quick plan to address the areas of improvement.

Visibly charting progress is another method for making learning visible. In short, this method requires converting student performance into a chart. It is often best to have stu-dents complete their own charts. Two examples of how teach-ers have used charting come from a writing class and a math class. In one elementary classroom, the teacher was encourag-ing students to write as much as possible during a five-minute freewrite at the start of the writing period. She noticed that many students were fearful of misspelling words and would not write very fluently. To encourage writing fluency, she had the students chart the number of words they wrote during each freewrite. Every few days, she gave the students a new goal. We provide an example of this fluency chart. A math teacher used a similar chart to help students keep track of how well they were learning their times tables. Every day he would give the students one minute to solve as many problems as they could. When they were done, he would have the students chart their progress.

Finally, another example of how to make a student's learn-ing visible is to show them their growth as visually and as concretely as possible. A simple way to do this is to save each student's work or to have students create and maintain a port-folio where they keep key selections of their work. As students work throughout the year, have them save drafts of work for larger projects as well as samples of similar kinds of work they complete over the year. By doing this, students are able to see and reflect on their growth and learning over the year. Elementary reading and mathematics teachers use a variety of software packages that support charting of student growth and improvement. However, important for building student-teacher relationship and motivation is the time spent in conferencing about this information.

One of the more creative ways we have seen a teacher help make a student's learning visible was by recording student participation. In one high school Spanish class, the teacher was encouraging students to participate in classroom discussions, particularly discussions where students were to speak in Spanish. The teacher would use a seating chart and record each time a student spoke during a discussion. Over the course of the year, the teacher would meet with students and show them how many times they were speaking and help the students set participation goals. Over the course of the year, many students were able to see their participation and confidence in speaking Spanish increase.

Figure 6.1   Sample Fluency Chart

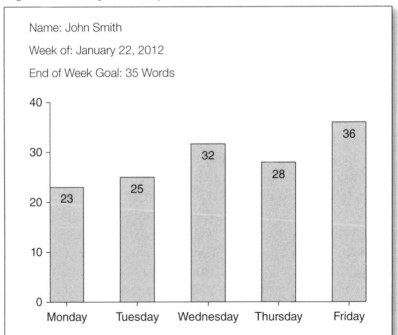

Teaching Students How to Ask for Feedback

As discussed in Chapter 5, feedback is one of the most effective strategies for supporting student motivation and achievement. However, feedback can be more effective when it targets and provides exactly what a student needs and is ready to hear (e.g., Anderson, 2000; Perks, 2005). Therefore, when preparing to give feedback, we encourage teachers to teach students how to request feedback. We often associate the practice of giving feedback to playing darts at night. When there is not a lot of light, it is very difficult to hit the mark; yet when things are clear and bright, we are more likely to get a bull's-eye. Similarly, unless a teacher has a solid understanding of what a student is working on, trying to accomplish, and having the most difficulty with, it is very difficult to determine what type of feedback will be the most helpful.

Dialogue Folders

Teaching students how to ask for feedback is a powerful way to develop strong teacher-student relationships. When teachers encourage students to talk about their work, they are encouraging the students to communicate their learning process. While students are doing this, the teacher is *listening*. Over time, such a pattern encourages students and teachers to form strong relationships grounded in the academic work of the classroom. For example, one strategy Kevin frequently used when he taught at the middle school and high school level was what he refers to as dialogue folders (Perks, 2005). The folders were a place for students to write to Kevin about their work and to submit excerpts or drafts for feedback. Kevin gave students specific prompts to use when writing to him (see three feedback prompts on next page). Every day or so, Kevin would read the folders and what students were saying. He would then write back and provide feedback based on their requests. Over the course of the year, the folders provided an artifact of the ongoing conversation the students were having with their teacher. Many of the students found the folders so valuable they asked to keep them at the end of the year.

Feedback Prompts

An effective way to make sure teachers have the information they need to give targeted and informative feedback that a student will use is to teach students how to ask for it. This may sound counterintuitive, but many students often need to be taught how to ask for feedback. Consider the times when students have asked you to look over or give feedback. It is likely they ask something like this: "Mr. Middleton, can you take a look at this and tell me what to fix?" Now compare this request to the following.

"Mr. Middleton, can you please give me some feedback on my lab report? I have finished my first draft and I think it is decent overall. However, I find it really hard to word the hypothesis and am not sure I am getting that part right. Also, I am not sure I have provided enough information at the end. What do you think?"

This type of request is much more helpful for a teacher. However, most students will not solicit feedback in this way unless they are taught how to do so.

There are various ways teachers can encourage students to begin discussing their work and learning. Anderson (2000) uses a simple cue when having miniconferences with elementary students about their writing. During writing time, he will work with one student at a time. When he sits or kneels next to a student, he begins the conversation by asking, "How's it going?" This is often enough for the students to begin talking about their work. Another, slightly more detailed approach, is to show students how to explain or describe important elements of whatever it is they are working on. For example, students could be taught and expected to communicate the following when requesting feedback.

1. Describe what you have been working on or what you are trying to accomplish.

2. Describe what is going well.

3. Describe what you have struggled with the most.

Simple questions such as these help ensure that the teachers have the information they need to determine what feedback to give.

Encouraging students to be as informative as possible when soliciting feedback also helps increase the likelihood that students will use the teacher's feedback. In the previous example, if the student had not provided the information she had, the teacher (a) may not have given feedback about the hypothesis statement or (b) the teacher may have provided feedback on something the students was not concerned or interested about. Additionally, the simple framework provided can also be phrased as questions when a teacher sits down with students to discuss their work. Before giving feedback, the teacher can ask the students what they have been working on and struggling with the most. The information provided will help the teacher decide what feedback will be most helpful. In doing so, the teacher increases the likelihood that students will find the information helpful. In addition, the teacher will also have demonstrated that he or she listened and cares about what the students have to say.

STRATEGIES FOR SUPPORTING POSITIVE PEER RELATIONSHIPS

The strategies and approaches described here are designed to help teachers encourage students to develop strong and positive relationships as they work and learn together. These evidence- and research-based strategies are grounded in various research studies on cooperative learning (e.g., Johnson, Johnson, & Holubec, 2008; Slavin, 1991; 1995) and have been selected because they can be used in a variety of situations with students at various age levels.

Establishing and Using Group Norms

Establishing group norms is a common tool adults use in collaborative and team environments to facilitate and help individuals engage in complicated work. Norms are typically a small set of rules that help guide how individuals should act with one another when engaging in work with peers. Sometimes individuals confuse norms with protocols. Whereas protocols identify steps within a process, norms describe principles that help individuals maintain positive relationships with each other, especially when the work is challenging or personal or both. Garmston and Wellman (1999) identify seven norms of collaboration.

1. Promoting a spirit of inquiry

2. Pausing

3. Paraphrasing

4. Probing

5. Putting ideas on the table

6. Paying attention to self and others

7. Presuming positive intentions

Additional norms that we have had success with include the following:

- Understand that those who work, learn.
- Phrase questions for benefit of all.
- Recognize that each person's ideas have value.
- Challenge ideas, not individuals.
- Share talk time.
- Read the group.
- Keep your goals in mind.
- Be present.

Norms work best when they are used whenever students work together in groups or engage in collaborative activities. One suggested use is to have a group of students review the norms at the beginning of every work session and to select one norm to focus on for that block of time. Toward the end of the work time, the group should spend a couple minutes debriefing how well they honored or met the norm. It is often helpful for the teacher to model or facilitate conversations about norms when they are first introduced to students. It is also important to keep in mind that the purpose of having norms is to encourage students to focus on the work at hand and the needs of their classmates. In short, they help promote a caring attitude toward the work and others.

Think-Pair-Share

Think-pair-share (Lyman, 1981) is a simple strategy that teachers commonly use to encourage students to develop cooperative discussion skills with other students in a low-stake context. This strategy can be used during any phase of instruction. It typically uses a simple three-step protocol. The first step often includes a prompt from the teacher, where he or she asks each student to think or consider a question or idea. Next, the teacher asks students to pair up (often with a student who is nearby) and share what they thought with their partners. The teacher can then walk around and listen to what the students are discussing. The final step is to have a few of the pairs share what they discussed with the rest of the class.

Think-pair-share is a useful strategy that can help students develop positive peer relationships because it provides students with opportunities to process and communicate information in a low-stakes context. We have seen teachers use this protocol at the start of a lesson to give students an opportunity to access prior knowledge, consider what they learned previously, or predict what they think they will be learning. The strategy also works in the middle of lessons or activities by giving students an opportunity to metacognitively reflect and discuss their progress and learning. Think-pair-shares are also great tools used to process and discuss learning after an activity has been finished.

Task Grouping Strategy

One strategy that we have developed to help design collaborative tasks and to effectively match students with other students for the task is what we call the *task grouping strategy*. This strategy encourages teachers to think about the nature of a task before determining how to organize students into groups. This strategy categorizes tasks into four different types. These are described next.

1. **Independent group task**—This type of task or activity encourages students to work independently. For example, some projects can easily be divided into multiple parts. When students work together in a group, they can divide and conquer without ever really working together. Often, the purpose of an independent group task is to enable students to complete a project that is too large for a single individual. An example of this type of task could be a presentation or slide show where each students works on their own slides and are only in charge of explaining these when it comes time for presenting.

2. **Parallel group task**—This type of task encourages students to work independently but in the presence and view of other students in the group. An example of this might occur in a math class when a teacher wants students to work in pairs to solve a problem but requires the students to solve the problem first before having the students compare their answers. The purpose of parallel group tasks is to provide students with the opportunity to observe other students in case they may struggle with the activity themselves. During such activities it is expected that students can observe and watch other students if and when they struggle.

3. **Cataloging task**—Cataloging tasks are more collaborative than the previous two types of tasks; however, they allow individual students to keep their personal work distinct from their classmates. The purpose of this type of task is to encourage students to work together by listening to and sharing one another's ideas without a great deal of response or feedback. An example of a cataloging task could be when an English teacher asks a group of students to analyze a poem and identify all of the literary devices. The students would work in a

group generating a list of what they see. However, this list would be the collection of each student's individual observations. It would be very easy to determine who contributed what during this type of task.

4. **Organic task**—This type of task is the most complicated type of task and requires the highest degree of comfort and trust. Organic tasks require students to work closely together and to combine their ideas into a unique and single product. Often, the product is greater than the sum of the parts. One example could come from an art class where the teacher is asking students to work together to use clay to create a bust of a famous person. To do this, one student might shape the nose. Once this was finished, another student might make some changes or alterations to the first student's work. Another example is when students work together to create a single piece of writing.

One of the key features of the four task types described here is that each type of activity requires a different level of collaboration and trust. Understanding these task types helps teachers design or modify tasks based on their understanding of how well a group of students work together. Often, collaborative groups fail because teachers unintentionally ask students to work at a level beyond their comfort zone. For example, they might ask students to work in an organic manner, when parallel or cataloging work would have been more appropriate. Matching students to the right type of task encourages students to build their skills of collaborating and working with others and, by doing so, build stronger relationships with their peers.

Student-Centered Text-Based Discussion Protocol

We developed the following protocol to help teachers foster student-centered discussions and help students learn how to have thoughtful conversations with one another about what they have read. This protocol can be adapted for use whenever students read complex texts in any discipline. This tool is particularly useful given the increased text complexity demands in the Common Core State Standards for English Language Arts and Literacy. Once students become comfortable with this protocol, the teacher can foster high-quality discussions with little effort. This protocol is designed to engender thoughtful conversations that support students' understanding of material. This protocol can be used after students have read a complete text or during reading of longer works to facilitate discussion about the reading. Here are the steps of the protocol.

STUDENT-CENTERED DISCUSSION PROTOCOL

1. **Preread**

   a. Engage in a prereading/prelearning activity (e.g., K-W-L Chart, anticipation guide, problematic situation, etc.)

2. **Read**

   a. Read text in class. The passage should be short (1 or 2 pages). If you are reading a longer work, select a passage that will act as a springboard for the discussion.

   b. Read aloud or silently—however, if reading aloud, have a competent reader read the entire passage.

3. **Generate Questions**

   a. After reading the text, ask the students to generate and share questions. Questions can focus on unfamiliar vocabulary or content. Record these questions on the board.

   b. Define any vocabulary before continuing.

4. **Reread**

   a. Have the students reread the text. Encourage them to consider the questions that were just asked as they read. Remind them that they will be discussing these questions soon.

5. **Discussion**

   a. After reading, pick a student to facilitate the discussion.

   b. The facilitator can pick any question on the board. She must answer it first. Then she can call on other students to respond.

   c. Some classes are able to engage in discussion without having a facilitator call on people. Use your discretion; however, too much interrupting silences students.

   d. The teacher can participate as well, just be careful not to dominate the discussion.

6. **Debrief**

   a. The teacher finally leads a discussion on how well the conversation worked. Good questions to ask are the following:

      i. How did it go? Why?

      ii. Why did some of you not speak?

Chapter Summary

As we mentioned at the beginning of this chapter, relationships really matter. They matter at home, at work, and in the classroom. As most of us know, building strong and durable relationships with students requires establishing an environment where students feel safe and comfortable to challenge themselves academically and take intellectual risks. It also demands consistent demonstrations of interest in students' lives, consistent opportunities for all individuals in the classroom to learn about one another by engaging in meaningful work, and ongoing feedback that helps students see and understand their progress.

An additional point to make in closing this chapter is that the other elements of motivation also work to help build strong and enduring relationships as a part of learning in school. This chapter is the last in Section II because of the strong connection between the other three chapters and relationship building. We strongly believe that strong, tight-knit communities that exhibit high levels of motivation and engagement develop when individuals work with purpose around common work. When we promote student voice, we send the message that we value students' opinions and their input in the classroom. When we strive to craft meaning-ful learning activities, we show students that we care about their interests and what they value. Finally, when we scaffold activities and learning so students can succeed on challenging tasks, we are setting high standards and also communicating confidence in their skills and abilities.

CHAPTER WRAP-UP ACTIVITY

The following activity is designed to help teachers consider and apply what they have read in this chapter. The purpose of the Rela-tionship Reflection Sheet is to help a teacher periodically (1) ana-lyze the relationships in the classroom, (2) develop strategies to strengthen or maintain relationships, and (3) reflect on the prog-ress of relationship building in the classroom. We encourage teach-ers to engage in this activity three or four times a year.

RELATIONSHIP BUILDING SHEET

Directions

The following table is designed to help teachers analyze the quality of relationships in the classroom and develop strat-egies to improve them. Begin by writing each student's name in the first column. Next, assess the strength of each student's relationship with you as his or her teacher, as well as with his or her peers. For example, you can use a scale from 1 to 5 with a "1" indicating a weak relationship and a "5" indicating a strong relationship. Next, based on how you assessed the relationship with each student, identify a strategy that could support one of the student's relationship needs. At the end of the quarter or semester, reflect and record notes about any improvements or changes in each student's relationship with you and others. Then, start the process over again.

Student Name	Teacher Relationship	Peer Relationships	Strategy	Reflection

SECTION III

Maintaining and Sustaining Motivation

INTRODUCTION

Section I of this book provided you with the opportunity to deepen your understanding and to reconceptualize motivation. The focus was on considering motivation as an ongoing, active force that can be accessed as a learner engages in meaningful work and that a teacher can learn to navigate to facilitate the learning process. However, for teachers, having some concrete strategies to enhance the motivational quality of their classroom is instrumental to creating successful learning. Section II addressed motivation to learn by focusing on four important motivation-related areas of focus for teachers to consider: fostering student voice, creating meaningful tasks, promoting challenge with success, and building positive relationships. In Section II, readers were also encouraged to self-assess their practice within those areas of focus and to consider a variety of instructional practices and strategies.

We now return to our initial analogy of motivation as a river current. The metaphors of motivation as a gas tank with students being "full" or "empty" of motivation and of a garden in which the right conditions will result in motivation do not fully reflect the complexity of classroom motivation as a process that happens over time and is the result of several factors including the student, teacher, instruction, curriculum, and the school and community setting. In thinking about motivation as a river current, we acknowledge that it is part of a journey that takes time to unfold. We also acknowledge that the teacher, as the navigator on this journey, needs to be skilled at using the current to move along in the journey with knowledge of how other factors, such as the weather, impact how to navigate successfully. In terms of the classroom, to transform motivational culture teachers should consider not only their instructional practices, as focused on in Section II, but also how motivation develops over time, how school and community values and beliefs about learning impact motivation, and how their engagement as professionals impact the climate of motivation in their classroom. For a rafter, learning basic paddling techniques is essential, but they become useful when they are employed in the context of an actual journey with the opportunities and challenges that are a part of every trip. The same can be said for teachers who desire knowledge of instructional techniques to transform classroom motivational culture but then need to enact those techniques over time with unique groups of children in their local context.

Section III widens the lens for examining motivation through classroom interactions between teachers and students by considering the larger professional and community context in which motivation and learning occur. Specifically, this section of the book is devoted to considering the relationships between motivation and a teacher's development, the school and community climate, and the role of time. Although strategies can be enacted in one moment in time, motivation is situated in a school community with a particular group of learners. In this section, we invite you to think about the teaching profession and the cultural context of teaching as you work to improve the motivational climate of your classroom.

Chapter 7 tackles the question of how a classroom culture of motivation can be built and sustained. As teachers, we may experience motivated activity as part of an activity or project but may also wonder how that motivation can be sustained and developed over time. This chapter will consider how a culture of motivation may experience ups and downs in its progression and how teachers can work with their students and in their schools over time to sustain that culture. Chapter 8 considers how teaching, and therefore motivation, is not an isolated activity within a single classroom but may affect and be affected by school and community cultures or the beliefs and values that surround us. Part of navigating the current of motivation is anticipating and learning to use or overcome the opportunities and challenges that come from the larger environment. Finally, Chapter 9 examines how teachers, through their professional development and motivation (not just instructional practices or dispositions), may contribute to transforming the classroom culture of motivation. The gas tank and gardening metaphors suggest focusing on how we can change students or how we can change the classroom; however, this chapter challenges teachers to think about becoming better navigators of the motivational energy or current in the classroom through a continual process of self-improvement and self-motivation.

7

Sustaining Motivation Over Time

I n the previous section, we presented examples of ways to develop practices and reinforce strategies for navigating the motivational energy or current in your classroom. However, culture is a set of practices, values, and beliefs that are fostered and sustained over time and across generations. As teachers, if we want to transform the motivational culture in our learning contexts, we must consider not only momentary changes that may contribute to the motivation for an activity around a certain task or project but also how that culture develops and can be sustained over time.

Case Study Revisited

In Chapter 1, we presented the case study of River View Middle School and highlighted students who portrayed different qualities of engagement across two classrooms. We now turn to a case study that illustrates the perspectives of teachers.

Mr. Julio Martinez has been teaching for several years, and Ms. Susan O'Brien is a new teacher at River View Middle School. They are on an interdisciplinary team together with two other veteran teachers. Both teachers have had positive feedback from their principal who conducted observations in the fall, but other than team meetings, they've had little opportunity to discuss their teaching with colleagues. Early in the spring of their first year, they are both leaving the building after working late to grade papers.

"How was your day, Susan?" asked Julio.

"Fine, Julio . . . just fine," she responded with hesitation. He waited for her to continue. "But I've really been struggling with a handful of students in my class. They're terrific kids, but I feel like some days I just don't know how to light a fire under them. One day we'll be moving along with an activity; they're working together and engaged. Then, the next day, I introduce a lesson that I've worked hard on, but they just sit and stare at me."

"What do you have them working on now?"

"Well, we're doing a unit on graphing on the x and y axis. We practiced for two days with rulers and number lines. The students even built their own graphs. But then when I gave them word problems to apply it today, they looked at me like I'm speaking a different language."

Julio nodded in agreement, "I struggled with the same issue in my first couple of years. But it wasn't with all my students. There were a few who'd participate in any activity we did, but it was always those same few hands. I know some of them just don't think they'll enjoy reading and writing and shut down when they come in my room. I still have days like that!"

Susan responded with surprise, "But I've been in your classroom. I see your students reading silently in the corner, building word maps on the wall, and editing each other's writing. They even talk about your class and their work in your class!"

"Well," Julio considered, "over time I was able to test ideas on what worked based on what they'd done in elementary school and what the students seemed interested in here. I brought in some books they were familiar with and even some books that are set in this town. I kept parents updated on our projects and know they talk about it at home because some of my first students have

younger brothers and sisters in class now. They seem excited to know what our big project will be for the year."

As she walked to her car, Susan held up a folder with student papers. "I just spent an hour grading their papers and don't see any progress. I have to think of something to do for tomorrow to get them motivated."

ACTIVITY 7.1 REFLECTION

How has your teaching developed over time, and what has been its impact on your students? Complete the chart by describing yourself and your students at different time points in your teaching. The time scale can be adjusted according to how long you have been teaching.

	Early Teaching	After Some Experience Teaching	Now
Description of Your Teaching			
Description of Your Students' Engagement			

Classroom Culture

Every classroom has its own culture. We have all been students, and many of us have been teachers in different classrooms. Your experience in each of those classrooms was likely very different because each classroom had its own unique culture. In this book, we are focused on classroom cultures in which students and teachers are productively engaged with meaningful, collaborative work and in which the work is indicative of the social practices, beliefs, and values shared in the classroom. A variety of factors help define the culture of a classroom. These include, but are not limited to, the following: (1) the values for learning, (2) the beliefs about how to learn, (3) the reasons and purposes for engaging in academic work, and (4) the rules about how to behave and work together.

Identifying representative moments within your classroom and understanding the reoccurring commonalities of those activities over time can provide insight into how your classroom's culture has been created and what might transform it. However, culture is not built from a single episode or a series of unconnected events. Classroom culture is a more enduring set of beliefs, values, and goals that dictate and guide the interpretation of classroom practices and activities. For example, in our case study of teachers, Mr. Martinez referred to the way he includes reading materials that are relevant to his students' lives, includes parents and the community as part of learning, and requires students to collaborate on work. An essential element of how he does this is by understanding and incorporating the assets, interests, and strengths students bring into the classroom.

In achievement goal theory, classroom culture is understood through classroom goal structures. Researchers (Ames, 1992; Kaplan et al., 2002; Meece, Anderman & Anderman, 2006) have found that there is often a prevailing message in classrooms that emphasizes the importance of developing and improving competence or the importance of demonstrating and proving competence. Based on the work of Ames (1992), our colleagues have identified important features of classrooms that contribute to the motivational culture. We listed those features in Chapter 1 and relist them here for you to consider within the context of understanding motivational culture.

Task: the manner in which teachers structure tasks and learning activities

Autonomy: the locus of responsibility in the classroom

Recognition: the appearance, purpose, and types of recognition used in the classroom

Grouping: how students are arranged to work together

Evaluation: the informal and formal ways students are assessed and evaluated

Time: how time is used to manage classroom activities

The features represented within TARGET can help teachers assess and better understand the nature of the motivational culture in their classroom. Next are several survey items (Midgley et al., 2000) that allow students to distinguish between classrooms that focus on mastery versus performance.

Although classroom culture may be thought of as the way a teacher designs a classroom through instruction, rules, and interactions, it is important to understand that students have just as much to contribute to the classroom culture. In fact, a secondary school teacher who teaches in the same room with the same curriculum and instructional strategies but who has different groups of students understands that two different classes are likely to have different cultures. Similarly, an elementary school teacher understands that each year her classroom may have a different culture depending on the students. There may be considerable overlap or similarities from year to year or from class to class because of what the teacher brings

Table 7.1   Survey Items Assessing Classroom Motivation Climate

Student Survey Items That Reflect a Mastery-Oriented Classroom	Student Survey Items That Reflect a Performance-Oriented Classroom
In our class, trying hard is very important.	In our class, getting good grades is the main goal.
In our class, how much you improve is important.	In our class, getting right answers is very important.
In our class, really understanding the material is the main goal.	In our class, it's important to get high scores on tests.
In our class, it's OK to make mistakes as long as you are learning.	

to the context, but culture, and motivational culture in particular, is shaped by all the participants and the work in which they jointly engage.

A year in a classroom, like a river journey, is a long process. The experience of that year depends in large part on the motivational climate that is established and sustained over time. There seems to be a consensus among many of the teachers we have talked with that the culture of a classroom forms very quickly and often within the first month or so of the school year. This is a time when social relationships are established, the interests and strengths of students become apparent, and the planning and instructional approaches of the teacher are made explicit. We strongly advocate for teachers to convey messages and engage in practices that emphasize student voice, growth and development, the meaningfulness of work, challenge with support, and caring.

Once a positive classroom motivational culture is established, teachers and students can then act in ways that sustain the culture. Challenges will certainly arise during any school year and sometimes hinder the motivated activity of the classroom. How the teacher and students navigate those challenges and reestablish their engaged work may depend on the prevailing culture. Again, this viewpoint suggests that we think about motivation not as the quality of an individual or a single successful instructional moment in a classroom. Instead, motivation is part of the underlying current of energy in a classroom, in which student participation may ebb and flow during their time in the classroom. Just as some rivers may be known for their deep, strong currents, classrooms may develop the same reputation for being a place where motivation is strong and consistently exhibited in the productive activity of the teacher and students despite challenges that arise.

Group Flow

Most teachers experience moments when the students in their classroom seem to be working harmoniously on a challenging, interesting activity. These are the moments that teachers such as Ms. O'Brien in our case study strive for and hope will define the culture of their classroom. In moments such as these, a teacher may be providing support to students who have questions, observing them collaborating in thoughtful productive ways, and may lose track of time or outside concerns. Csikszentmihalyi (1990, 1996) described times such as these as moments of "flow" where individuals experience high levels of challenge, cognition, engagement within a task, and pleasant emotions at completion. The experience of high school students was shown to fluctuate in and out of flow states depending on the nature of the activity they were engaged in (Shernoff, Csikszentmihalyi, Schneider, & Shernoff, 2003). This suggests that the development of a culture of motivation may ebb and flow as students and teachers engage in a variety of activities throughout the day or year. As with the flow of a river current, fluctuation in flow seems inevitable since it is a function of not just the content but the instructional format and qualities of the individual.

Moments of flow are not only a phenomenon that individuals experience, but they may also occur as an experience of "group flow" (Sawyer, 2008) among a group of individuals working together, such as you and your students in the classroom. Sawyer (2008) suggests this may happen among a group when skills match the challenge, the goal is clear, immediate feedback is provided, and there is freedom to fully concentrate on the activity. Many teachers and learners may have had the experience of being fully engaged in concentration and collaboration during a classroom activity only to look at the clock and be amazed how quickly the time passed.

ACTIVITY 7.2 REFLECTION QUESTIONS

1. Identify a time you experienced group flow as a teacher or a student.

2. Describe your experience. Where did it happen?

3. Who was present?

4. What were you working on?

5. What feelings did you experience during and after?

6. Were there things that your teacher, or you as the teacher, did to facilitate or sustain that feeling of group flow? What did the other participants do to facilitate or sustain group flow?

Signature Practices

Many teachers who are able to foster and sustain classrooms with cultures of high motivation and engagement develop what we refer to as "signature practices." These signature practices are instructional events or learning activities that integrate many of the practices described in Section II and illustrate the motivational possibilities that are present in the classroom. They often become part of a teacher's reputation as well. These events may be tied to an academic project (e.g., a mock trial, a play), an ongoing activity or project (e.g., math competition, the 2nd grade model of the community, National History Day, or collecting data on local plants as citizen scientists) or an instructional practice that is used across several activities (e.g., collaborative team learning, project-based learning). The shared features of these types of signature practices include a commitment to deep learning, enacting motivational beliefs such as the ones explored in Chapters 3 through 6, and their public, ongoing nature. Signature practices may be a repeated learning activity within a classroom across years, or they may have some variation from year to year. In either case, they serve to build a motivational climate in which students enter the classroom with positive regard and allow their qualities of motivation to emerge.

We have encountered many wonderful examples of signature practices in our work. For example, when asked if he enjoyed school, a sixth grader from a local middle school responded that he did, but continued that he could not wait for eighth grade when he would be able to participate in the Civil

War reenactment that a social studies teacher held every year. This activity evolved over several years and became something many students eagerly anticipated as they entered eighth grade. It was based on the teacher's strong content knowledge of that historical era and tied to demonstrating local and state content standards. Another example of a signature practice comes from a high school where we have worked with a team of teachers who developed an interdisciplinary unit in which students read *A River Runs Through It* by Norman McLean and learn about river ecology. The teachers also teach the students how to flyfish, and the unit culminates in an overnight flyfishing trip. An example of a signature practice we have witnessed in an elementary school is a school post office where students create and operate an interclassroom postal service all year long. The students love it.

The concept of signature practices has been most often described by school-level events. In *Visionary Middle Schools* (Morocco, Brigham, & Aquilar, 2006), the authors describe how local innovation in instruction based on a common activity or practice could be pointed to in several schools that were experiencing successes that exceeded expectations. The signature practices in the schools they examined ranged from interdisciplinary work to exhibitions and technology to investigations. In all cases, these practices became common goals and expectations for teachers and students and led to innovation and learning. Just as the Pygmalion Effect, described earlier in the book, demonstrated that a teacher's expectation for individual students can result in higher achievement, the presence of a signature practice that assumes participation and learning from each student may have the same effect on a group. Thus, tapping into the motivational current or energy of students can begin before they even step into the classroom through reputation and anticipation.

Another example of signature practices at the school level is from the professional development organization Expeditionary Learning Schools (EL; www.elschools.org). On their website, EL states their goal to "develop leadership capacity across the school to build a shared vision for school transformation and a professional culture rooted in quality, continuous improvement and trust." The learning expeditions in EL schools engage students in real-world issues through fieldwork, inquiry, service learning and long-term projects. In an EL school, students at each grade level expect to engage in rich, challenging expeditions that "energize student motivation and engagement through high-level tasks and active roles in the classroom." Some examples of learning expeditions from the EL website include the following.

> *High school.* An examination and report by 10th graders of whether the staircases in their urban neighborhood are safe, an inquiry that required deep understanding of mathematical principles such as slope.

> *Middle school.* The creation of a *Life in a Vernal Pool* field guide by 7th graders to address standards in ecology, taxonomy, and art as well as mastering skills in nonfiction reading and writing.

> *Elementary school.* The construction and maintenance of garden plots by 1st graders to engage in standards in life science, economics, and nutrition.

ACTIVITY 7.3 REFLECTION ACTIVITY

Visit the Expeditionary Learning Schools' website as a way to review and consider more examples of local signature practices. Choose one or two learning expeditions to examine. How do those examples use specific practices and strategies described in Chapters 3 through 6 of this book? Identify specific strategies and how they were used in service of the larger project.

In our work with schools, we can identify a number of classrooms where a signature practice has become the expectation and provides a similar motivational energy through which the teacher and students may engage in demanding, meaningful work (see Table 7.2).

Our witnessing of classrooms and schools where signature practices have grown and flourished has provided evidence of the ongoing motivation that can occur when teachers establish activities based on principles, practices, and strategies described earlier in the book, such as developing voice or autonomy (Chapter 3), creating meaningful tasks (Chapter 4), providing challenge with supportive structures to succeed (Chapter 5), and building positive relationships (Chapter 6).

Three important elements of the signature practices we have observed are important to mention. First, most practices take time to build. Teachers' initial efforts often point out challenges that must be overcome for a signature practice to become a motivational phenomenon for a classroom; persistence was key. Second, the teachers who built these signature practices used established educational theory and research to guide their decision making in how to create these projects. Third, the signature practices were only one

Table 7.2   Additional Examples of Signature Practices

1. A local first grade classroom engages in a "picturing writing" curriculum (www.picturingwriting.org) that enhances literacy through art.
2. A group of local fifth grade teachers developed a math skill-building activity using football statistics and team competitions.
3. A middle school in the area has a three-day hike/camping event for eighth grade students that focuses on personal challenge and collaboration.
4. Each spring a local middle school engages children in a fitness challenge that culminates in a running event focusing on personal challenge and improving performance, not speed or winning.
5. An area high school requires that each graduating student complete a senior project in which they identify, complete, and present an inquiry project based on their interests under the guidance of an advisor.

part of the classroom year. The dedication, focus, and energy required for these practices are considerable and often could not be sustained throughout a year. Although these practices emerged as salient moments in defining the motivational climate of a classroom, they were embedded in and supported by yearlong curricula. They can occur several times each year or once each year, but require intensive planning by teachers, deep engagement of students, and involvement of the community for public exhibit.

CHAPTER SUMMARY

This chapter explored the notion of classroom culture and motivation. By classroom culture, we refer to the shared beliefs, values, goals, and social practices of a classroom. Although a teacher may develop skills and activities to facilitate motivation, the culture of a classroom comes from different sources—the teacher, the learners, and the nature of the activities they engage in. Some motivational theories, such as achievement goal theory and flow theory, have provided descriptions of a motivated classroom in action as well as the qualities of such classrooms and the experiences of the participants.

We also emphasized that a classroom culture of motivation is not built on a single learning activity or series of unrelated activities. Early in the year, a classroom culture seems to emerge from the different sources described. When that motivational climate is established, there are ways the teacher can contribute to its sustainability, just as a river guide can work with a river current to facilitate a journey.

Finally, the chapter explored the notion of signature practices, or a repeated learning activity that requires deep engagement, collaboration, and sometimes the public exhibition of work. Such signature practices at the classroom or school level may tap into the motivational energy of students before they even enter the classroom in anticipation of this shared, meaningful work.

ACTIVITY 7.4 APPLICATION TO PRACTICE

How would you define a signature practice? Think about the examples provided in this book or develop examples from your experiences or work with others. Those examples could be existing practices or ideas that could be developed into a signature practices.

Next, develop a concept map for a possible signature activity. In Figure 7.1, we provide some beginning features of your concept map to help you start. How are these elements fulfilled and connected to each other? What other elements are needed and how are they connected?

Figure 7.1

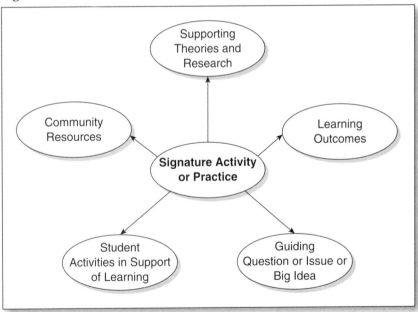

8

The Social Context of Motivation

I n the Chapter 7, we explored the notion of classroom culture as a way to understand how motivation is developed through the intersection of teacher, student, and curriculum and how that culture may be sustained over time as activities evolve to meet the strengths and interests of students, including collaboration for deep learning, and products that are publicly exhibited. One highlight was the notion of signature practices within a classroom or across a school. However, teachers often face a broader climate or environment that challenges their actions and may create roadblocks to implementing practices that have a competing or coordinating impact on transforming classroom culture.

CLASSROOMS AND CONTEXT

Although teachers may operate independently from day to day in their classroom, their efforts exist within the social systems of cultures and norms that prevail in the broader contexts of schools and communities. Figure 8.1 displays the relationship of classrooms as embedded in these larger social systems. As part of a complex social system, the work we do in classrooms both reflects and contributes to the schools, communities, and cultures within which we work. Our instructional approaches, curriculum choices, and relations with students and families are often a reflection of the nature of these different social systems, their values, beliefs, and social practices. Therefore, accessing the motivational energy of students may depend on the larger cultures in which a classroom exists, much like navigating a river current depends not only on features of the river (depth, speed, and obstacles) but also features of larger systems such as weather, animal and plant life, and construction.

Figure 8.1   Layers of Social Context Influencing Classroom Motivation

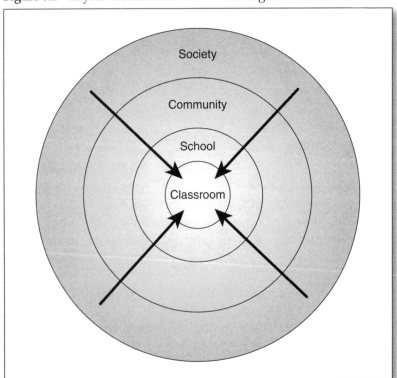

ACTIVITY 8.1 CRITICAL REFLECTION

What do you see as obstacles and opportunities outside the classroom to enhancing the motivational climate of your classroom at each level?

	Obstacles	Opportunities
School		
Community		
Culture		

The Role of Societal Culture

In *Multicultural Education,* Banks and Banks (2010) define culture as "the shared beliefs, symbols, and interpretations within a human group" (p. 8). They continue to state that the "essence of a culture is not its artifacts, tools, or other tangible cultural elements but how the members of the group interpret, use, and perceive them. It is the values, symbols, interpretations, and perspectives that distinguish one people from another in modernized societies" (p. 8). Culture is pervasive in our beliefs, values, and actions to the extent that we often lose awareness of its presence and impact. As members of a culture, we may share beliefs about motivation that are reflected in the ways our classrooms operate, including both teacher and student values and behaviors.

It is important to note that cultures, including classroom cultures, may include subcultures of individuals for whom the prevailing cultural paradigm is contrary to their own culture, potentially leading to their resistance. In the case of motivational culture, it is important to note that resistance is not lack of motivation but rather motivation for different goals and purposes, as explored in Chapter 1. For example, Giroux (2001) advocates for active participation in a culture of resistance when the predominant culture emphasizes and replicates what he describes as oppressive and antidemocratic tendencies including the increasing "corporatization" of schooling. Similarly, Ogbu (2003) suggests that the racial achievement gap in the United States is not due to a lack of motivation or ability but represents a resistant culture in minorities whose ancestors were brought to this country involuntarily and who see achievement in schooling as aligned with behaviors and attitudes of majority culture. Therefore, trying to succeed in school for members of these groups would require partial abandonment of one's own culture. Three examples of the impact of culture on teaching and learning may provide some clarity on its relation to motivation.

Markus and Kitayama (1991) described the divergent views about how Western and Eastern cultures view the self in relation to others. They compared Western cultures, which value the self over others, self attainment, and individuality to Eastern cultures, in which harmonious interdependence, group attainment, and attending to others are more valued. A cultural difference in the role of the self as independent versus interdependent may translate into the way our classrooms operate. The value of independence would lead to promoting individual success, even at the expense of the progress and achievement of others, and establishing assessment systems that highlight individual accomplishment. Achievement motivation in such a cultural setting may become focused on individual demonstration of success.

Another example of the way culture may relate to motivation is the portrayal of teachers in media within a culture. Swetnam (1992) examined the media distortion of the teacher image, particularly in comparison to other professions. She outlined several concerning images such as learning should always be easy and fun, teachers and students have an antagonistic relationship with principals, and the portrayal of teachers either as incompetent or as superhuman. As a result of these television and movie images, students in schools may hold attitudes about teachers and learning that can impact the motivational quality of how they approach school.

The impact of culture on motivation in the classroom is reflected in national policies as well. The United States has developed what some consider a "testing culture" (Moses & Nanna, 2007), in which tests are used for deciding educational opportunity, allocating funding, and determining instructional approaches. These authors further suggest that even though many may not like standardized tests, they are accepted as part of schooling rather than accepted because they are legitimate. Such a culture of testing is also concerning because of its replication of social inequities by racial and economic groups and by gender. When success is measured by standardized testing and instruction is developed with the sole focus on test performance rather than research-based principles of quality instruction, the impact on motivation may be quite dramatic.

ACTIVITY 8.2 REFLECTION

Consider how the culture in which you live relates to your classroom practices.

1. List several instructional practices you routinely use in the classroom. Put a checkmark next to those that reflect a value of independence and a star next to those that value interdependence. What does this tell you about your classroom culture?

2. Consider conversations you have had with individuals outside of the classroom. Have you experienced or witnessed times when noneducators supported or challenged traditional stereotypes of schools and teachers?

3. List classroom and instructional practices you have changed or adopted specifically because of the demands of the "culture of testing." How have those changes impacted the motivational climate of your classroom?

The Role of Community

The culture of a local community can also influence the culture of classrooms. For example, One Minneapolis, One Read is a "community-driven effort with individuals, neighborhood groups, educators, businesses and nonprofits all coming together" (www.oneminneapolisoneread.com) in an effort to promote literacy and dialogue throughout the community. In this initiative, one book is chosen and advertised in an effort to get as many community members as possible to read it. The book reflects an issue of importance in the community, such as an inspiring autobiography of a local individual overcoming challenges to become educated, to encourage community dialogue as well as literacy. A series of public forums to promote conversation are also planned. This community program illustrates how a community's beliefs and values about learning may impact motivation in classrooms.

In this context of our exploration of motivation and culture, we refer to community as a diverse group of people living in a common area with shared interests. Often, this is a neighborhood, town, city, or section of a city. Community involvement through businesses, universities, volunteer organizations, and government agencies may provide a variety of benefits to schools such as organized efforts to promote student wellbeing, job preparation, and maintaining a healthy community (Sanders, 2003). The presence or absence of community support and value for schools may relate to tangible benefits or obstacles for motivating students through partnerships or the motivational goals and aspirations for students within schools.

The relation of community value for schools and student outcomes may be particularly important for students from traditionally underachieving groups. For example, LaFromboise Hoyt, Oliver, and Whitbeck (2006) found community support to be a protective factor for Native American youth living near reservations and to be positively related to prosocial outcomes. Although we may often think of community involvement in schools as focused on mentoring/tutoring programs, financial or service contributions, and attendance at school events, LaFromboise's work describes community members' efforts to create a life-skills curriculum to prevent suicide in Native American youth based on community practices, assets, and values. So community involvement may be broadly conceived in its vision, purpose, and implementation.

Communities may enact a shared set of beliefs and values about learning in many ways. In a recent class at the university level, some of our students were asked to conduct an informal community inventory regarding youth and education. Here are some initiatives they identified:

- Library sponsored events for children
- Presence of a children's museum within a short driving distance
- Afterschool programming for children
- Afterschool academic enrichment or support programs for children
- Organized youth sports programs
- Community access to technology through local library
- Mentoring program for youth through community volunteers
- Local scholarships for higher education through community organizations
- Access to advanced learning within the local community or nearby

Even this short list illustrates the variety of ways communities interact with schools and classrooms.

Classrooms and schools exist within communities that hold values and provide community resources that can either promote or diminish motivation for achievement. For example, in some of our recent research (Middleton, Dupuis, & Tang, 2013), we found that indigenous youth interpreted messages from their community and integrated them into their motivational beliefs and goals. Some youth who would need to leave their local community to continue into secondary school but did not want to leave purposefully underperformed on the gateway tests into high school. Their motivation was also related to economic opportunity in their community. Some students who knew they would be limited in career options in their community held strong aspirations for schooling; whereas, others who believed they could survive while remaining in their community, often through subsistence farming, placed less value on advancing in school.

ACTIVITY 8.3 APPLICATION

Conduct an informal inventory of your community, using an Internet search if needed. List some community structures or activities that involve the community in schools. How do you think each item impacts motivation at the classroom level? How is access open or limited to all students who may benefit?

Community Activity Related to Local Schools	Impact on Motivation in Classrooms	Description of Access for All Students

---

The Role of Schools

Most classrooms exist within a school that has its own unique climate regarding learning and motivation. Cohen and his colleagues (2009) refer to school climate as being based on patterns of people's experiences of school life and reflecting norms, goals, values, interpersonal relationships, teaching and learning practices, and organizational structures (p. 182). . . . a positive school climate includes norms, values, and expectations that support people feeling socially, emotionally and physically safe (p. 182).

School climate has many facets—for example, social, athletic, and academic. Although all are interrelated to form a coherent larger school culture, each can be considered distinctly. Shouse (1996) explored the opportunity and tension between the social and academic missions of schools. A frequent concern is that the social cohesion of a school, including shared activities and caring relationships, is emphasized at the expense of academic culture, such as expectation and enforcement of high standards. In his study, Shouse found that a strong combination of emphasis on "communality" and emphasis on academics was the greatest predictor of achievement. Other conclusions in his study included that the social and academic emphases were closely related, that academic emphasis had its strongest impact on low socioeconomic schools, and that communality without academic emphasis did not result in achievement.

In moving from classroom to classroom, hearing school messages, viewing what achievements are celebrated, and participating in school events, students live and participate in a school culture every day. They also perceive what is valuable and important for the school and may adjust their beliefs and behaviors in accordance with those values. Teachers, as well, exist in the culture of their school and may find ways to participate or resist that culture through the way they teach, the content they include, the curriculum they offer, and how they participate in school governance.

ACTIVITY 8.4 CRITICAL REFLECTION

What are examples of "emphasis on communality" and "emphasis on achievement" in your school?

What messages are being communicated in these examples?

Do any of these messages contradict each other?

Are any of these messages directed to some students and not others? Who? Why?

Aligns With or Contradicts?	Emphasis on Communality	Emphasis on Achievement

---

Teachers as Buffers to School Motivational Climate

As mentioned in Chapter 1, students are able to perceive the motivational climate of their classroom and the achievement goals that are emphasized (Kaplan, Middleton, Urdan, & Midgley, 2002; Meece, Anderman, & Anderman, 2006). Although there is less research on the topic of school motivational climate, it is very possible that students also interpret and adjust their beliefs and behaviors according to their perception of what is emphasized in their school. Teachers may have concerns when their classroom strategies and practices that promote motivation, as were outlined in Chapters 3 to 6 (i.e., alternative methods of assessment, inquiry-based learning, or eliminating ability grouping), are in conflict with accepted practice or beliefs in the school.

Our students encounter many different demands from their surrounding environment. It is likely that the demands of the school may, at times, not align with the demands of the classroom. In outlining a theory of human motivation and behavior, Murray (1938) labeled these environmental demands as "presses." In his examination of a variety of environmental presses, he believed that the press experienced at the most proximal level was the most significant press driving behavior. In the case of schools and classrooms, teachers can take heart that the activities they engage in may be strongly salient to their students in developing their motivations, beliefs, and behaviors.

A recent study examined high school students' perceptions of performance goals, which are associated with problematic educational beliefs and behaviors, and specific classroom qualities that mitigate or "buffer" those negative effects (Ciani et al., 2010). Results suggest that in classrooms where there was a strong emphasis on community and classrooms in which teachers provided students opportunities to exercise their autonomy, the negative effects of performance goals were diminished. In other words, through their instructional approaches and by creating a positive classroom environment, teachers make a positive contribution to their students' motivation.

In sum, we suggest that the practices and strategies outlined in Chapters 3 through 6 can work to counteract school, community, and cultural environments that diminish motivation. So Figure 8.1 can be revised as depicted in Figure 8.2 to show the pushback, resistance, or contribution of classroom motivational culture to the different levels of environment. Teachers may experience a culture of testing in the larger society or community, but may choose to deemphasize the role of testing in their classrooms. Similarly, in a highly competitive community culture, a teacher may choose to develop more collaborative activities that rely on interdependence to promote learning and achievement. In doing so, these teachers become positive agents for change. Although there may be resistance by some students in the classroom, these buffering activities may serve as examples of successfully motivated classrooms that demonstrate deep student learning and engagement and may, as a result, shape beliefs and values in the school or community.

Figure 8.2   Bidirectional Impact of Social Context for Classroom Motivation

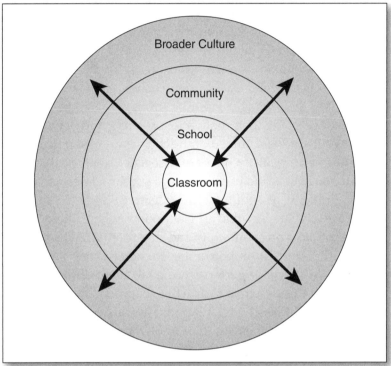

ACTIVITY 8.5 THEORY INTO PRACTICE

Revisit Figure 8.2. Consider each of the layers or circles and describe some elements within each of the levels that impact motivation in your classroom and how motivation in your classroom may serve to mitigate any negative demands of the environment to enhance motivational qualities.

Pushback to Culture	Pushback to Community	Pushback to School Climate

Teachers as Agents of Change

In their 2009 study mentioned earlier, Cohen and his colleagues (2009) explored not only positive school climate, but policies and practices that contribute to climate. The authors take the strong stand that if schools do not follow policies that promote positive school climate, which leads to a host of beneficial outcomes such as motivation, then schools are not meeting their obligation to students. As teachers, we are called on not only to work with students in our classrooms but also to contribute to the governance and policies of our schools to promote positive school climate.

Michael Fullan (1993) made a compelling argument for why teachers must act as agents of change and for the role of teacher education programs to foster leadership qualities in their graduates. He casts teaching as a moral activity, and because teachers have close knowledge of their students, they are in the best position to advocate for meaningful change. As this chapter has outlined in suggesting cultural change as a way to promote motivation, Fullan warns that "to restructure is not to reculture" (p. 16). We take his statement as advice to teachers to pay attention not only to changes in restructuring schools, but in the substance of those restructuring efforts to align them, in the case of our work, with principles of motivation and learning.

Regarding student motivation, teachers play a central role in "reculturing" their schools and communities by advocating for policies and practices that may promote positive motivational climates. Martin Maehr and Carol Midgley, in *Transforming School Culture* (1996) described their efforts to work directly with schools through the participation of teachers and administrators in conversations about affecting change in motivation and achievement in their schools. Their book details that experience and provides examples of advocacy for minimizing the emphasis on performance and proving competence in school while promoting a culture of intrinsic worth and developing and improving competence. The subsequent success of these schools serves as a model of teachers as agents of change in promoting practices and policies that improve motivation. The teachers and parents from the schools in Maehr and Midgley's book also developed a list of strategies for moving toward a more adaptive motivational culture in schools (See Table 1.2 in Chapter 1).

Many of the policies listed in Table 1.2 being advocated by Maehr and Midgley (1996) question long-standing traditions and practices in schools. Many teachers, parents, and students cannot envision their school without an honor roll or minimizing competition between students. Others who advocate for increasing voice for teachers and students in decision making and moving toward thematic approaches to curriculum may fit naturally into this vision for schooling. As with the practices and strategies described in Chapters 3 through 6, this book is not a to-do list for teachers. As advocates for change, you have the best understanding of your local context (e.g., the community, students, policymakers, opportunities, and limitations). You also have an awareness of your strengths as a teacher and leader within your school. Advocating for change requires taking those elements into consideration as you plan the best steps and strategies for improving the motivational climate of your classroom and school.

Chapter Summary

In this chapter, we explored how our classrooms are situated within larger social systems of schools, communities, and broader societies. These larger social systems provide schools with assets in people, ideas, and resources that can play a role in transforming classroom culture. There are also times when larger social systems may have qualities that conflict with a positive motivational culture at the classroom level. For example, many teachers have decried the "culture of testing" that they experience as limiting creativity and engagement in their classroom. We advocate for teachers to act as a buffer from forces outside the classroom that are potentially disruptive to motivation and to take a role as teacher leaders to advocate for practices that enhance motivation in their classrooms and schools.

ACTIVITY 8.6 CRITICAL REFLECTION

A consortium of leading organizations in education developed the Teacher Leader Model Standards (http://www. teacherleaderstandards.org) across several key domains. Place yourself along the continuum of beginning, developing, and mastering for each domain of leadership by providing evidence in the appropriate cell. Detailed standards for each domain can be found at the standards website. In the last column, brainstorm two to three actions you can take to move along the continuum.

Domain	Beginning	Developing	Mastering	Next Steps
Fostering a Collaborative Culture to Support Educator Development and Student Learning				
Accessing and Using Research to Improve Practice and Student Learning				

(Continued)

(Continued)

Domain	Beginning	Developing	Mastering	Next Steps
Promoting Professional Learning for Continuous Improvement				
Facilitating Improvements in Instruction and Student Learning				
Promoting the Use of Assessments and Data for School and District Improvement				
Improving Outreach and Collaboration With Families and Community				
Advocating for Student Learning and the Profession				

9

Maintaining
Self-Motivation

The demands placed on teachers are substantial and varied. Teachers are expected to plan, conduct classes, assess students, support students' academic and personal needs, collaborate in teams, inform parents, contribute to the governance of their school, and engage in professional development. According to The National Commission on Teaching and America's Future (NCTAF; Carroll, Fulton, & Doerr 2010), workload, lack of planning time, and lack of input into school policies have contributed to increasing teacher attrition rates across the country. Nearly half of new teachers do not stay in the profession beyond their fifth year. The economic, social, and academic costs of teacher turnover are substantial. Although the turnover rate varies by district, poorer schools face greater attrition rates. Moreover, according to the MetLife Survey of the American Teacher (MetLife Inc., 2012), which was endorsed by the American Association of Colleges for Teacher Education (AACTE), there has been a serious decline in teachers' satisfaction with their profession.

Although teacher retention is a complex issue with many contributing factors, one area to explore is teacher motivation. It seems likely that principles of motivation applied to students in classrooms may be applied to teachers to engage them in developing and improving as professionals. Our goal in this chapter is to identify some key motivational principles and corresponding activities that will support the growth of teacher motivation.

ACTIVITY 9.1 SELF-ASSESSMENT

To develop a sense of your motivation for improving and developing competence as a teacher, indicate how true the following statements are for you using the following scale.

1 = Not True at All	3 = Somewhat True	5 = Very True

_____ I have a plan for my professional growth and update that plan regularly.

_____ Over time, I find that my interest in what I teach continues to grow.

_____ I seek opportunities for professional development and continuous learning.

_____ I work with colleagues to build a professional learning community to improve teaching and learning throughout our school.

As you read each of the following sections, keep your responses in mind as a way to understand qualities of your motivation and areas on which you might focus.

Teacher Interest and Mastery of Content

As with students, an interest in subject matter and intrinsic motivation for studying the content is an indicator of motivation in teachers. Considerable research has explored teachers' content knowledge (e.g., Ball, Thames, & Phelps, 2008), and an emphasis on developing content knowledge is emphasized in teacher education programs. For example, the Council for Accreditation of Educator Preparation (CAEP), the accrediting body for teacher education programs, includes the following as its first standard for programs: "Candidates demonstrate an understanding of critical concepts and principles in their discipline" as well as "the pedagogical content knowledge necessary to engage students' learning of concepts and principles in the discipline" (Council for Accreditation of Educator Preparation, 2010). However, little attention has been given to teachers' interest in what they teach. It is assumed that a teacher chooses to teach in a content area of interest; however, little research exists to examine the development of teachers' interest in content.

From research on students, we know that interest is related to motivated behaviors such as persistence in developing competence and the likelihood of pursuing additional content knowledge. However, cultivating teacher interest in the subject matter is challenging. Many teachers, particularly elementary teachers, teach subject matter across several disciplines, typically language arts, mathematics, social studies, and science. Even secondary teachers who teach only one subject area are usually an expert or have passion about one area (e.g., American literature or ancient cultures) but need to teach the whole discipline to their students. Entering the classroom with such broad-based interest to encompass all areas being taught is unlikely.

For teachers, engagement with content knowledge should extend beyond the bounds of schools. Continuing education in content area courses, participation in the application of content into a variety of settings, and developing personal resources such as books, articles, and DVDs would contribute to motivation. This developing interest then provides more resources to students. However, the greatest resource is the teacher herself. Long and Woolfolk Hoy (2006) found that students' perceptions of a teacher's interest in content predicted their interest. Ongoing engagement with content is one way to build the motivation of a classroom by building the motivation of the teacher.

Pedagogical Motivation Knowledge

Even teachers with strong content knowledge and successful teaching skills can struggle finding the right way to channel students' motivation and learning toward a specific concept or set of concepts for all students. As the CAEP standard suggests, teachers should also demonstrate an understanding of pedagogical content knowledge. In moving from a novice to expert teacher, teachers often identify specific instructional practices and activities that seem to be engaging and meaningful learning opportunities for their students. This time-tested understanding of the effectiveness of certain teaching practices for particular subject matter content has been labeled pedagogical content knowledge (PCK; Shulman, 1986). PCK describes the intersection of content knowledge and pedagogical knowledge in which a teacher understands effective ways to promote student learning of specific content using strategies, examples, and activities particularly suited for that content. Teachers with strong PCK seem to have an understanding of how to represent subject matter, anticipate students' current knowledge and challenges to understanding, and a strong perception of how the learning environment or context impacts learning (Ball, 2000; Munby, Russell, & Martin, 2001; Shulman, 1987).

Although most of the work on PCK has focused on finding effective instructional practices for cultivating student understanding, it can be thought of as a way to consider effective practices for enhancing student engagement and the motivational climate of the classroom—a pedagogical motivation knowledge. PCK depends on the teacher's understanding of students' prior knowledge in making instructional choices; it assumes students can learn and do have knowledge. Similarly, pedagogical motivation knowledge requires the teachers to understand the motivational and affective qualities that students bring into the classroom and make instructional choices that build on those student qualities; it assumes students can learn and have motivation—our two underlying assumptions about motivation discussed in Chapter 2.

As teachers, we may often have a solid understanding of which activities "are working" with our students based on our experience and reflection. Although this PCK may develop in teachers over time, it is also a function of effective professional development (NPEAT, 2003) in which teacher reflective practice that focuses on context, instructional strategies, and subject matter as they are enacted in classrooms promotes more effective teaching. Shulman (1992) referred to this as the pedagogical reasoning cycle that involved several activities critical to good teaching:

Comprehension—understanding what you teach

Transformation—adapting materials to fit students' characteristics

Instruction—the variety of teaching actions required in the classroom

Evaluation—checking for understanding

Reflection—critically assessing one's own teaching

New comprehension—revised understanding of what you teach, how you teach it, and who you teach

This cycle of pedagogical reasoning overlaps with our notation of taking a WARM (watchful, adaptable, reflective, and modest) stance to translating teaching beliefs into action as key to transforming motivation culture. The notion of changing a single instructional practice or project as a way to enhance motivation is replaced in this approach to thinking about continual adjustments in navigating the motivational current that exists in your students and classroom.

ACTIVITY 9.2 CRITICAL REFLECTION

Consider how Shulman's notion of pedagogical content knowledge can translate into pedagogical motivation knowledge. Identify three effective strategies linked to motivation that you have or could use in your classroom. Then apply Shulman's pedagogical reasoning cycle to track how you reused those strategies through transformation, evaluation, and reflection.

Motivational Strategy	Was it successful?	Did you reuse it?	What did you change about it and why?

Teacher Self-Efficacy

In Chapter 1, we explained that self-efficacy is the belief in one's capability to succeed at the task at hand when effortful. Teachers may feel efficacious about at least three aspects of their work: the ability to impact student engagement and success, their classroom management, and their instructional abilities. In addition to self-efficacy, teachers may experience a sense of collective efficacy, the judgment whether the teachers in their school can be effective with their students and promote students' success.

The positive benefits of strong self-efficacy have been consistent across research studies and include higher job satisfaction, greater effort, increased motivation, and more resilience (Goddard et al., 2000; Labone, 2004). Others have found that self-efficacy increases in teachers early in their career then stabilizes at midcareer (Klassen & Chiu, 2010). It seems that teachers who have confidence in their effectiveness as teachers when they put effort into their work display benefits related to their beliefs, behaviors, and longevity as teachers. There are few teacher qualities that are consistently related to student achievement outcomes, but teachers' sense of efficacy is one of them (Woolfolk & Hoy, 1990).

There are a variety of pathways for teachers to build positive efficacy. Certainly, engaging in high-level, effective professional development is an important step for enhancing a sense of competence. Karabenic and Conley (2011) found that most teachers were highly motivated to participate in professional development and most have had positive experiences with it. The teachers in their study reported, on average, that their professional development work improved student competence and motivation. New teachers may also experience questions and a threat to their self-efficacy once they enter the classroom when faced with the daily challenge of teaching. Advanced studies for teachers, including both inservice development and out-of-school study, such as university coursework and professional association workshops, may provide opportunities to test and refine ideas and strategies for teaching and learning while trying to put those strategies into practice.

The National Comprehensive Center for Teacher Quality (2011) has outlined key aspects of high-quality professional development, including alignment with state and district standards and goals, modeling of teaching strategies for content, active learning, collaboration among teachers, embedded follow-up, and continuous feedback. By assuming that all students can learn and are motivated, as teachers we become more open to professional development opportunities ourselves. These qualities can be supported by taking a watchful, adaptable, reflective, and modest stance toward these opportunities, as outlined in Chapter 2, as a way to promote motivation. By taking such a stance, teacher efficacy may be enhanced. Moreover, the possibilities of change and achievement through specific targeted opportunities may provide a cycle of success in which those targeted activities provide feedback to teachers about what works in their classrooms leading to engagement in further targeted professional development opportunities (see Figure 9.1).

Figure 9.1   Cycle of Motivation for Professional Development

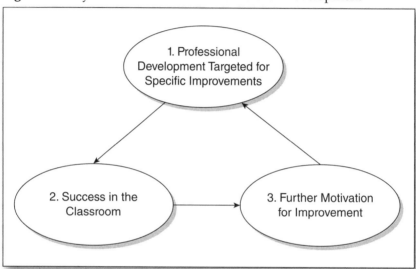

Establishing a Strong Professional Community

Just as students' connection to one another and their teachers relates to motivation, teachers also need to develop strong professional relationships. Getting along with other teachers contributes to problem solving and creating a shared work plan. As mentioned in Chapter 2, teachers not only feel a sense of efficacy for their work, but join with colleagues to develop a sense of collective efficacy (Goddard et al., 2000). Just as student motivation is more than the quality of an individual and the environment, teacher motivation is similar. The river guide depends on a community of professionals to help channel into the motivation current by relying on their expertise about things such as weather conditions, latest technologies, and previous experience on the river. Similarly a teacher needs to believe that the team of professionals working together on behalf of their students is capable of success. Teaching, like learning, is a group activity—not an individual activity.

Although the vast majority of the schools we have encountered have a dedicated faculty that work with one another with the goals of promoting student learning and wellbeing, in some places teachers have reported their experiences in schools in which students are viewed as problems, change is seen critically, new ideas are dismissed through anecdotal evidence, ideas for change or problem solving are infrequently shared, and distrust is evident (Deal & Peterson, 1998). Just as learned helplessness (Diener & Dweck, 1978) leads children to abandon effort and belief in their ability to succeed, negative attitudes and diminished sense of personal and collective efficacy may lead teachers to withdraw effort and hold skeptical beliefs about change.

In their book *Shaping School Culture: The Heart of Leadership,* Deal and Peterson (1998) suggest that in places where they exist, negative professional attitudes can be countered by actively recruiting more positive staff, celebrating the improvements and positive elements of a school, confronting negative attitudes head-on, and maintaining a focus on the learning mission of a school. It becomes the responsibility of all professionals in a school to begin turning a negative culture into one that embraces change and professional learning. Telling stories of success and improvement as well as pointing out opportunities that specifically address the mission of the school may be ways to begin this process. With colleagues and new teachers, we often advise them to find the like-minded professionals in their schools. We approach our work in schools with assumptions similar to those we hold for students: All teachers are capable of success in teaching, and all teachers are motivated. New professionals enter the field of teaching to make a difference, and accessing the current of motivation is essential in creating a culture focused on improvement and development.

More formally, many educators have turned to a professional learning community (PLC; Astuto, Clar, Read, McGee, & Fernandez, 1993) either within a school or with colleagues outside school in which teachers and principals seek opportunities for continual improvement by shared learning as an effective approach to teaching development. Dufour and colleagues (Dufour, Eaker, & Many, 2006) highlighted the critical elements of PLCs, including a focus on improving student learning and experience, collaboration, investigation/inquiry, evidence-based decision making, and a commitment to continuous improvement. This shared work can build trust among teachers when it engages the full faculty in activities and discussions related to the school, makes new teachers feel welcome, supports opportunities for collaboration, and improves communication (DuFour et al., 2006). In fact, several resources have emerged through technology to support this process. The website www.allthingsplc.info focuses on information and opportunities about PLCs for educators; the website also provides blogs and forums to begin the creation of such a community online.

In working with preservice teachers, we often encourage them to seek formal and informal mentors in their school. Engaging with colleagues in positive conversations about students, teaching, and learning is a good first step. It is also important to build relationships with teachers who share similar values and beliefs about the direction of your school and the nature of teaching. Positive relationships focused on the outcomes of student motivation and learning lay the groundwork for innovative practice, collaboration, valuing shared work, and persistence in problem solving, all markers of motivation in the classroom. Professional relationships can also be found outside the school through professional organizations such as the National Council of Teachers of English (NCTE), National Council of Teachers of Mathematics (NCTM), and other national and regional professional groups that hold annual conferences and local meetings.

Finally, just as students need an appropriate level of challenge and the support to meet those challenges, teachers also need this balance of challenge and support. Teachers face many challenges in their work—planning, managing, and assessing students. Those challenges may be a threat to motivation when they are seen as too difficult to overcome or hopeless. In finding solutions to challenges, teachers also need to hold the WARM stance described earlier toward their practices to help refine and improve those practices.

One method we have found particularly helpful in challenging and supporting teachers is involvement in Critical Friends Groups (CFG; www.nsrfharmony.org). CFG grew out of an Annenberg Institute for School Reform initiative to promote practices that lead to student achievement. These groups meet at least once per month for two hours and typically include 5 to 10 teachers. CFG meetings follow a specified protocol of presentation, critical conversation, questioning and feedback, reflection, and action plans. The participants of CFGs agree to shared norms of collaboration, shared responsibility for improving teaching and learning, and reflective dialogue.

FINAL THOUGHTS ON PROFESSIONAL DEVELOPMENT

In his analysis of more than 800 studies of what works in education, Hattie (2009) concluded that teachers are a strong force in the process of student learning. This was especially true for teachers who have engaged in high-level professional development. The process of school improvement would be simple if highly experienced, high-performing teachers could be hired for each classroom. However, new generations of teachers need to be recruited, trained, and developed to meet the continual need for effective teachers. Hattie identified essential themes for professional development with the strongest impact:

- Extended over a long period
- Effective use of external experts
- Teacher engagement in developing learning and skills
- Challenging teacher assumptions and perceptions about learning

- Communication among teachers about teaching
- School leadership facilitate and support of professional development

We encourage teachers and school leaders to consider these when creating opportunities for professional development in their contexts.

CHAPTER SUMMARY

In this chapter, we explored the way in which motivational principles—interest, efficacy, support, and relationships—can be applied not only to students but also to teachers. Teachers can take individual actions to enhance their knowledge and pedagogical content knowledge as a pathway to building motivation in the classroom. Engagement in specific activities to improve our teaching may build a positive cycle of motivation in which informed improvements lead to success, and that feedback furthers the desire for improvement. In sum, we encourage teachers to proactively find positive professional communities built on a mission of improving motivation and learning.

Conclusion

In this third section of the book, we tried to reinforce the notion that motivation is situated in the context of schools and cultures at a particular moment in time. Motivation is a dynamic current running through our classrooms that may be used to navigate the teaching and learning process to improve student results. However, practices and strategies for transforming a classroom motivation culture may run contrary to contextual factors; the teacher can serve as a buffer to diminish a negative impact of outside factors on student motivation and focus on their approach. This work is not easy and requires attention to teachers' motivation to teach, which can be supported through developing interest, relationships, and a sense of efficacy for teaching.

The metaphors of motivation as a gas tank—a fixed quality of individuals—or as a garden—in which elements of a classroom dictate motivation—are problematic and lead to stagnation rather than transformation. By considering only the learner as in control of motivation creating an external locus of control, teachers may feel a diminished sense of efficacy and believe that nothing they do can change the student. Moving to the garden metaphor, teachers may develop the belief that creating motivation is as easy as adding sunlight and water to get a garden to grow. They may then get frustrated and exhausted when their best efforts at adding a new incentive system or fun activities do not result in sustained motivation. Although curriculum and strategies are essential to transforming school culture, change is not that simple and needs to consider the broader context of time, place, assets, and opportunities.

Finally, we presented you with the notion of motivation as a river current that always exists and can be accessed or leveraged as part of the journey of a classroom. As teachers, we need to remember that the current always exists and to believe in the purpose of the journey. With those assumptions in place and with a deep understanding of the strengths, abilities, preferences, and motivations of their students, teachers can learn to navigate the complex conditions that surround them in the classroom.

We believe that each of you—with a WARM stance, broad knowledge of instructional strategies, and a deep understanding of your students and context—can transform your classroom into a culture of motivation and learning.

ACTIVITY 9.3

We invite you once again to complete the grid of a Frayer Model and compare it to the grid you completed at the beginning of the book to track the development of your learning and understanding of motivation.

(Continued)

(Continued)

Frayer Model	
DEFINITION of MOTIVATION	CHARACTERISTICS
EXAMPLES/MODELS	NONEXAMPLES

Appendix

Strategy and Practice List

Strategy/Approach/Practice	Chapter
4WH Framework	Promoting Student Voice
Capstone Projects	Designing Meaningful Tasks
Communicating Clear Learning Objectives	Promoting Challenge With Success
Connecting Students to Experts and Professionals	Designing Meaningful Tasks
Democratic Governance	Promoting Student Voice
Demonstrations and Think Alouds	Promoting Challenge With Success
Dialogue Folders	Building Positive Relationships
Entrance Tickets	Promoting Student Voice
Exit Ticket	Promoting Student Voice
Feedback Prompts	Building Positive Relationships
Feedback Questions	Promoting Student Voice
Fist to Five	Promoting Student Voice
Fluency Charts	Building Positive Relationships
Four-Phase Model of Interest Building	Designing Meaningful Tasks

(Continued)

(Continued)

Strategy/Approach/Practice	Chapter
Green Light Survey	Promoting Student Voice
Group Norms	Building Positive Relationships
Guidelines for Clear Directions	Promoting Challenge With Success
Keep Your Word	Building Positive Relationships
Knowledge Rating Charts	Promoting Challenge With Success
Linking Classroom Work to Students' Goals	Designing Meaningful Tasks
Making Learning Visible	Building Positive Relationships
Models and Exemplars	Promoting Challenge With Success
Preassessments	Promoting Challenge With Success
Project-Based Learning	Promoting Student Voice
Putting It in Writing	Building Positive Relationships
Referencing Learning Objectives	Promoting Challenge With Success
Relevance Mapping	Promoting Challenge With Success
Service Learning	Promoting Student Voice
Simulating Work Outside of School	Designing Meaningful Tasks
Student-Centered Discussion Protocol	Building Positive Relationships
Task-Grouping Strategy	Building Positive Relationships
Think-Pair-Share	Building Positive Relationships
Three-Minute Writing	Promoting Challenge With Success
Time to Write	Promoting Challenge With Success
Value-Oriented Questions	Promoting Challenge With Success

Glossary of Key Terms

Choices—Options that teachers give to students in an attempt to promote student voice

Classroom culture—The values for learning, beliefs about how to learn, reasons and purposes for engaging in academic work, and the rules about how to behave and work together experienced in a classroom

Collaborative learning—An instructional approach that encourages students to collaborate with teachers on instruction and assessment where students may help to set goals, coplan, make decisions about processes and strategies, and ultimately accept responsibility for products and learning outcomes—also includes coguiding group processes and helping to facilitate activities

Engagement—The attention, behaviors, and efforts indicating involvement in a learning activity

Feedback—Information provided to individuals about their work and progress that they can use to improve and regulate their learning

Flow—Moments when individuals experience high levels of challenge, cognition, and engagement within a task, and pleasant emotions at completion; **Group flow**—the experience of flow among a group of individuals working together

Formative assessment practice—Informal methods of gathering data about and providing feedback to students about their learning during classroom instruction

Instructional feedback—Refers to information students give a teacher about instruction that can help the teacher improve teaching practices

Learning objectives—Specific outcomes of learning that measurably define what students are expected to be able to do and know

Mastery goal—Engaging in academic work for the purpose of developing or improving competence

Meaningful learning—Learning that individuals want to engage in because it is perceived as being interesting, useful, or having social value

Mindset—The way an individual views and or approaches specific tasks. (An individual with a *fixed* mindset believes that his or her abilities tend to be fixed or non-malleable and will determine success on a given task. Individuals with a *growth* mindset believe that abilities can improve and are the product of effort and growth.)

Motivation—The energy that can lead to activity or engagement directed toward a goal; motivation to learn is the activity between students and teacher as they engage in the work of their classroom

Optimal challenge—Tasks that are well matched to a student's knowledge and skills and are perceived by the student to be meaningful, as well as not too easy and not too hard

Pedagogical content knowledge—The intersection of content knowledge and pedagogical knowledge in which a teacher understands effective ways to promote student learning of specific content using strategies, examples, and activities particularly suited for that content

Pedagogical motivation knowledge—Knowledge that requires the teachers to understand the motivational and affective qualities that students bring into the classroom and make instructional choices that build on those student qualities

Performance goal—Engaging in academic work for the purpose of demonstrating or proving competence

Self-Efficacy—A learner's belief about his or her competence on a task; **Collective efficacy**—The judgment or belief that the group of teachers in a school can be effective with their students and promote student success

Signature practice—A repeated learning activity that requires deep engagement, collaboration, and sometimes the public exhibition of work; such signature practices at the classroom or school level may tap into the motivational energy of students before they even enter the classroom in anticipation of this shared, meaningful work

Student voice—Refers to opportunities students have to shape and influence decisions in their learning

Task value—The importance placed on succeeding at a task based on interest in, importance of, or utility of the task

Teacher stance—The way in which teachers prepare to act in accordance with their beliefs

References

Alexander, P. A. (1997). Mapping the multidimensional nature of domain learning: The interplay of cognitive, motivational, and strategic forces. In M. L. Maehr & P. R. Pintrich (Eds.), *Advances in motivation and achievement* (Vol. 10, pp. 213–250). Greenwich, CT: JAI.

Ambrose, S. A. (2010). *How learning works: seven research-based principles for smart teaching* (1st ed.). San Francisco, CA: Jossey-Bass.

Ames, C. (1992). Classrooms: Goals, structures and student motivation. *Journal of Educational Psychology, 84*(3), 261–271.

Anderman, E. M., & Anderman, L. H. (2010). *Classroom motivation* (1st ed.). Upper Saddle River, N.J.: Pearson.

Anderson, C. (2000). How's it going? A practical guide to conferring with student writers. Portsmouth, NH: Heinemann.

Anderson, R., Green, M., & Loewen, P. (1988). Relationships among teachers' and students' thinking skills, sense of efficacy, and student achievement. *Alberta Journal of Educational Research, 34*(2), 148–165.

Armstrong, T. (2009). Multiple intelligences in the classroom (4th ed.). Alexandria, VA: Association for Supervision and Curriculum Development.

Aronson, J., & Steele, C. (2005). Stereotypes and the fragility of academic competence, motivation and self-concept. In A. J. Elliot & C. S. Dweck (Eds.), *Handbook of Competence and Motivation* (pp. 436–456). New York, NY: Guilford Press.

Ashton, P. T., & Webb, R. B. (1986). Making a difference: Teachers' sense of efficacy and student achievement. New York, NY: Longman.

Assor, A., Kaplan, H., & Rotj, G. (2002). Choice is good, but relevance is excellent: Autonomy-enhancing and suppressing teacher behaviours predicting students' engagement in schoolwork. *British Journal of Educational Psychology, 72,* 261–278.

Astuto, T. D., Clar, A. M., Read, A. M., McGee, K. & Fernandez, L. (1993). *Challenges to dominant assumptions controlling educational reform.* Andover, Massachusetts: Regional Laboratory for the Educational Improvement of the Northeast and Islands.

Baker, J. A. (1999). Teacher-student interaction in urban at-risk classrooms: Differential behavior, relationship quality and student satisfaction with school. *The Elementary School Journal 100*(1), 57–70.

Bagnall, N., & Cassity, E. (2012). *Education and belonging.* New York, NY: Nova Science.

Ball, D. L. (2000). Bridging practices: Intertwining content and pedagogy in teaching and learning to teach. *Journal of Teacher Education, 51*(2), 241–247.

Ball, D. L., Thames, M. H., & Phelps, G. (2008). Content knowledge for teaching: What makes it special? *Journal of Teacher Education, 59*(5), 389–407.

Bandura, A. (1986). Social foundations of thought and action: A social cognitive theory. Prentice-Hall, Englewood Cliffs, NJ.

Banks, J. A., & Banks, C.A. (2010). *Multicultural education: Issues and Perspectives* (7th ed.). Hoboken, NJ: John Wiley and Sons.

Barron, B., & Darling-Hammond, L. (2008). *Powerful Learning: What We Know About Teaching for Understanding.* San Francisco, CA: Jossey-Bass

Black, A. E., & Deci, E. L. (2000). The effects of instructors' autonomy support and students' autonomous motivation on learning organic chemistry: A self-determination theory perspective. *Science Education, 84,* 740–756.

Bong, M. (2004). Role of self-efficacy and task value in predicting college students' course performance and future enrollment intentions. *Contemporary Educational Psychology, 26*(4), 553–570.

Brookfield, S. D. (1995). Becoming a critically reflective teacher. San Francisco, CA: Jossey Bass.

Brookhart, S. M. (2010). How to assess higher-order thinking skills in your classroom. Alexandria, VA: ASCD.

Buehl, D. (2001). *Classroom strategies for interactive learning.* Newark, DE: International Reading Association.

Card, D. E., Giuliano, L., & National Bureau of Economic Research. (2011). *Peer effects and multiple equilibria in the risky behavior of friends.*

[NBER working paper series working paper 17088] Retrieved from, http://www.nber.org/papers/w17088

Carroll, T. G., Fulton, K., & Doerr H. (Eds.). (2010). *Teaming up for 21st century teaching and learning*. National Commission on Teaching and America's Future. Retrieved from, www.nctaf.org/wp-content/uploads/2012/01/TeamUp-CE-Web.pdf.

Chiu, M. M. (2000). Group problem solving processes: Social interactions and individual actions. *Journal for the Theory of Social Behavior, 30*(1), 27–50, 600–631.

Ciani, K. D., Middleton, M. J., Summers, J. J., & Sheldon, K. M. (2010). Buffering against performance classroom goal structures: The importance of autonomy support and classroom community. *Contemporary Educational Psychology, 35*, 88–99.

Clark, A. E., & Lohéac, Y. (2005). *"It wasn't me, it was them!" Social influence in risky behavior by adolescents*. [Discussion paper no 1573] Retrieved from, http://www.iza.org/en/webcontent/publications/papers/viewAbstract?dp_id=1573

Cohen, J., McCabe, L, Michelli, N.M., & Pickeral, T. (2009). School climate: Research, policy, teacher education and practice. *Teachers College Record, 111*(1), 180–213.

Cotterell, J. (2007). *Social networks in youth and adolescence* (2nd ed.). New York, NY: Routledge.

Cornelius-White, J. H., & Harbaugh, A. P. (2010). *Learner-centered instruction: building relationships for student success*. Thousand Oaks, CA: Sage.

Council for Accreditation of Educator Preparation. (2010). CAEP 2013 Standards for accreditation for teacher preparation. Retrieved from, http://caepnet.org/accreditation/standards/.

Csikszentmihalyi, M. (1990). *Flow: The psychology of optimal experience*. New York, NY: Harper and Row.

Csikszentmihalyi, M. (1996). *Creativity: Flow and the psychology of discovery and invention*. New York, NY: Harper Perennial.

Csikszentmihalyi, M. (2005). Flow. In A. J. Elliot & C. S. Dweck (Eds.), *Handbook of competence and motivation* (pp. 598–608). New York, NY: The Guilford Press.

Danielson, C. (2006). Teacher leadership that strengthens professional practice. Alexandria, VA: ASCD.

Deal, T. E., & Peterson, K. D. (1998). *Shaping school culture: The heart of leadership*. San Francisco, CA: Jossey-Bass.

Deci, E. L., & Ryan, R. M. (2002). Self-determination research: Reflections and future directions. *Handbook of self-determination research.* (pp. 431–441). Rochester, NY: University of Rochester Press.

Demanet, J., & Van Houtte, M. (2004). Teachers' attitudes and students' opposition: School misconduct as a reaction to diminished effort and affect. *Teacher and Teacher Education, 28*(6), 860–869.

Diener, C. I., & Dweck, C. S. (1978). An analysis of learned helplessness: Continuous changes in performance, strategy and achievement cognitions following failure. *Journal of Personality and Social Psychology, 36*(5), 451–462.

Downey, G., Eccles, J. S., & Chatman, C. (2005). *Navigating the future: Social identity, coping, and life tasks.* New York, NY: Russell Sage Foundation.

Dufour, R., Dufour, R., Eaker, R., & Many, T. (2006). *Learning by doing: A handbook for professional learning communities at work.* Bloomington, IN: Solution Tree.

Durik, A. M., Vida, M., & Eccles, J. S. (2006). Task values and ability beliefs as predictors of high school literacy choices: A developmental analysis. *Journal of educational psychology, 98*(2), 382–393. doi: 10.1037/0022–0663.98.2.382

Dweck, C. S. (2006). *Mindset.* New York, NY: Random House.

Dweck, C. S. (2008). *Mindset: The new psychology of success.* New York, NY: Ballantine Books.

Eccles, J. S. (2005). Subjective task value and the Eccles et al. model of achievement-related choices. In A. J. Elliot and C. S. Dweck (Eds.), *Handbook of Competence and Motivation* (pp. 105–121). New York, NY: Guilford Press.

Eccles, J. (2009). Who am I and what am I going to do with my life? Personal and collective identities as motivators of action. *Educational Psychologist, 44*(2), 78–89.

Eccles, J. S., & Midgley, C. (1989). Stage/environment fit: Developmentally appropriate classrooms for early adolescents. In C. Ames & R. Ames (Eds.), *Research on motivation in education* (Vol. 3, pp. 139–186). New York, NY: Academic Press.

Epstein, J. (1989). Family structures and student motivation: A developmental perspective. In C. Ames & R. Ames (Eds.), *Policies for America's public schools: Teacher equity indicators* (pp. 89–126). Norwood, NJ: Ablex.

Ertmer, P. A., & Simons, K. D. (2005). Scaffolding teachers' efforts to implement problem-based learning. *International Journal of Learning, 12*(4), 319–328

Erwin, J. C. (2004). *The classroom of choice: giving students what they need and getting what you want.* Alexandria, VA: Association for Supervision and Curriculum Development.

Eyler, J., & Giles, D. (1999). *Where's the learning in service-learning?* (1st ed.). San Francisco, CA: Jossey-Bass.

Farrell, T. S. C. (2004). *Reflective practice in action.* Thousand Oaks, CA: Corwin.

Finkel, E., & Fletcher, S. (April 2002). The portfolio/colloquium to certify competence and assess program goals: Balancing program requirements and assessment with candidates' experiences. Paper presented at the Annual Meeting of the American Educational Research Association, New Orleans.

Fisher, D., Frey, N., & Lapp, D. (2009). *In a reading state of mind: brain research, teacher modeling, and comprehension instruction.* Newark, DE: International Reading Association.

Fletcher, A. (2002). FireStarter youth power curriculum: Participant guidebook. Olympia, WA: Freechild Project.

Fullan, M. G. (1993). The complexity of the change process. In M.G. Fullan (Ed.), *Change forces: Probing the depth of educational reform,* (pp. 19–41). Philadelphia, PA: Falme Press.

Francis, B., Skelton, C., & Read, B. (2012). *The identities and practices of high-achieving pupils: Negotiating achievement and peer cultures.* New York, NY: Continuum.

Gardner, H. (1999). Intelligence reframed: Multiple intelligences for the 21st century. New York, NY: Basic Books.

Garmston, R. J., & Wellman, B. M. (1999). *The adaptive school: a sourcebook for developing collaborative groups.* Norwood, MA: Christopher-Gordon.

Gee, J. P. (2003). What video games have to teach us about learning and literacy. New York, NY: Palgrave Macmillan.

Giroux, H. (2001). *Theory and resistance in education.* Englewood Cliffs, NJ: Praeger.

Goddard, R. D., Hoy, W. K., Woolfolk, A. (2000). Collective teacher efficacy: Its meaning, measure, and effect on student achievement. *American Education Research Journal, 37*(2), 479–507.

Goodenow, D., & Grady, K. E. (1993). The relationship of school belonging and friends' values to academic motivation among urban adolescent students. *The Journal of Experimental Education,* 62(1), 60–71.

Grant, C. A., & Sleeter, C. E. (2007). *Doing multicultural education for achievement and equity.* New York, NY: Routledge.

Guay, F., Ratelle, C. F., & Chanal, J. (2008). Optimal learning in optimal contexts: The role of self-determination in education. *Canadian Psychology, 49,* 233–240.

Halaby, M.. (2000). *Belonging: creating community in the classroom.* Cambridge, MA: Brookline Books.

Hamre, B. K., & Pianta, R. C. (2006). Student-teacher relationships. In K. M. Minke (Ed.), *Children's needs III: Development, prevention, and intervention* (Vol. 10, pp. 59–71). Washington, DC: National Association of School Psychologists.

Hare, W. (2006). Humility as a virtue in teaching. *Journal of Philosophy of Education, 26*(2), 227–236.

Hattie, J. (2009). Visible Learning: A synthesis of over 800 meta-analyses relating to achievement. New York, NY: Routlege.

Hattie, J. (2012). Visible learning for teachers: Maximizing impact on learning. New York, NY: Routledge

Hebert, T., & Durham, S. (2008). *High-stakes teaching: practices that improve student learning.* Lanham: Rowman & Littlefield Education.

Heritage, M. (2013). *Formative assessment in practice: A process of inquiry and action.* Cambridge, MA: Harvard Education Press.

Hickey, D. T. (2003). Engaged participation versus marginal non-participation: A stridently sociocultural approach to achievement motivation. *Elementary School Journal, 103,* 401–429.

Hidi, S., & Renninger, K. A. (2006). The four-phase model of interest development. *Educational Psychologist, 41*(2), 111–127.

Hidi, S., Renninger, K. A., & Krapp, A. (2004). Interest, a motivational variable that combines affective and cognitive functioning. In D. Y. Dai & R. J. Sternberg (Eds.), *Motivation, Emotion, and Cognition: Integrative Perspectives on Intellectual Functioning and Development* (pp. 89–115). Mahwah, NJ: Erlbaum.

Iyengar, S., & Lepper, M. R. (2000). When choice is demotivating: Can one desire too much of a good thing? *Journal of Personality and Social Psychology, 79*(6), 995–1006.

Jang, H., Reeve, J., & Deci, E. L. (2010). Engaging students in learning activities: It's not autonomy support or structure, but autonomy support and structure. *Journal of Educational Psychology, 102*(3), 588–600.

Jennings, P. A., & Greenberg, M. T. (2009). The prosocial classroom: Teacher social and emotional competence in relation to student and classroom outcomes. *Review of Educational Research, 79*(1), 491–525.

Johnson, D. W., Johnson, R. T., & Holubec, E. J. (2008). *Cooperation in the classroom* (8th ed.). Edina, MN: Interaction Book Co.

Juvonen, J., & Wentzel, K. R. (1996). *Social motivation: Understanding children's school adjustment.* Cambridge, NY: Cambridge University Press.

Kaplan, A., Middleton, M., Urdan, T., & Midgley, C. (2002). Achievement goals and goal structures. In C. Midgley (Ed.), *Goals, goal structures, and patterns of adaptive learning.* Hillsdale, NJ: Erlbaum.

Karabenick, S. A., & Conley, A. (2011). Teacher motivation for professional development, math and science partnership-motivation assessment program. University of Michigan, Ann Arbor, Michigan. Retrieved from, http://mspmap.org/wp-content/uploads/2012/01/Teacher- 0PDM.pdf.

Katz, I., & Assor, A. (2007). When choice motivates and when it does not. *Educational Psychology Review, 19*(4), 429–442.

Klassen, R. M., & Chiu, M. M. (2010). Effects on teachers' self-efficacy and job satisfaction: Teacher gender, years of experience, and job stress. *Journal of Educational Psychology.* 102, 741–756.

Kolb D. (1984). *Experiential learning: experience as the source of learning and development.* Englewood Cliffs, New Jersey: Prentice Hall.

Labone, E. (2004). Teacher efficacy: Maturing the construct through research in alternative paradigms. *Teaching and Teacher Education, 20,* 341–359.

LaFromboise, T. D., Hoyt, D., Oliver, L., & Whitbeck, L. (2006). Family, community, and school influences on resilience among American Indian adolescents in the upper Midwest. *Journal of Community Psychology, 34,* 193–209.

Lemov, D. (2010). *Teach like a champion.* Hoboken, NJ: John Wiley & Sons.

Long, J. F., & Woolfolk Hoy, A. (2006). Interested instructors: A composite portrait of individual differences and effectiveness. *Teacher and Teacher Education, 22*(3), 303–313.

Lyman, F. (1981). The responsive classroom discussion: The inclusion of all students. *Mainstreaming Digest.* College Park, MD: University of Maryland.

Maehr, M. L., & Midgley, C. (1996). *Transforming school cultures.* Boulder, CO: Westview Press.

Markus, H. R., & Kitayama, S. (1991). Culture and the self: Implications for cognition, emotion, and motivation. *Psychological review, 98*(2), 224–253.

Marzano, R. J. (2003). *What works in schools: Translating research into action.* Alexandria, VA: Association for Supervision & Curriculum Development.

Marzano, R. J. (2006). *Classroom assessment and grading that work.* Alexandria, VA: Association for Supervision & Curriculum Development.

Marzano, R. J. (2009). *Designing & teaching learning goals & objectives.* Bloomington, IN: Marzano Research Laboratory.

Marzano, R. J. & Marzano, J. S. (2003, September). The key to classroom management. *Educational Leadership, 61*(1), 6–13.

McCaslin, M. (2009). Coregulation of student motivation and emergent identity. *Educational Psychologist, 44*(2), 137–146.

McClelland, D. (1985). How motives, skills and values determine what people do. *American Psychologist,* 40, 812–825.

McCombs, B. (2010). Learner-centered practices: Providing the context for positive learner development, motivation, and achievement. In J. L. Meece & J. S. Eccles (Eds.), *Handbook of research on schools, schooling, and human development* (pp. 60–91). New York, NY: Routledge.

McKeachie, W. J. (1995). Learning styles can become learning strategies. *The National Teaching and Learning Forum, 4*(6), 1–3.

Meece, J. L., Anderman, E. M., & Anderman, L. H. (2006). Classroom goal structures, student motivation, and academic achievement. *Annual Review of Psychology,* 57, 487–503.

Meltzer, J., & Jackson, D. (Eds.). (2010). *Thinkquiry toolkit I.* Portsmouth, NH: Public Consulting Group.

Mendler, A. N. (2000). *Motivating students who don't care: Successful techniques for educators.* Bloomington, IN: National Educational Service.

MetLife, Inc. (2012). Survey of the American teacher: Teachers, parents and the Economy. Retrieved from, https://www.metlife .com/assets/cao/contributions/foundation/american-teacher/ MetLife-Teacher-Survey-2011.pdf.

Meyer, D. K., Turner, J. C., & Spencer, C. A. (1997). Challenge in a mathematics classroom: Students' motivation and strategies in project-base learning. *The Elementary School Journal, 97*(5), 501–521.

Middleton, M. J. (2004). Motivating through challenge: Promoting a positive press for learning. In P. R. Pintrich & M. L. Maehr (Eds.), *Advances in Motivation and Achievement, Vol. 15.* (pp. 209–232). Amsterdam, The Netherlands: Elsevier JAI Press.

Middleton, M. J., Abrams, E., & Seaman, J. (2011). Self-regulatory reflective practice in teacher education: Resistance and dis-identification. *New Directions on Teaching and Learning, 126,* 67–76.

Middleton, M. J., Dupuis, J., & Tang, J. (2013). The development of motivation and academic identity for science learning in early adolescents from indigenous communities. *International Journal of Science and Math, 11*(1), 111–141.

Middleton, M. J., & Midgley, C. (2002). Beyond motivation: Middle school students' perception of press for understanding. *Contemporary Educational Psychology, 27,* 373–391.

Middleton, M. J., Seaman, J., Rheingold, A., & Tang, J. (April 2012). *Examining the situated nature of academic press in middle school small-group interactions.* Paper presented at the Annual Meeting of the American Educational Research Association, Vancouver, BC.

Midgley, C. (Ed.). (2002). Goals, goal structures, and patterns of adaptive learning. Mahwah, NJ: Erlbaum.

Midgley, C., Feldlaufer, H., Eccles, J. (1989). Change in teacher efficacy and student self- and task-related beliefs in mathematics during the transition to junior high school. *APA, 81*(2), 247–258.

Midgley, C., Maehr, M. L., Hruda, L. Z., Anderman, E., Anderman, L., Freeman, K., Gheen, M., et al. (2000). *Manual for the pattern of adaptive learning survey (PALS).* Ann Arbor, MI: University of Michigan.

Miller, S. D. (2003). How high- and low-challenge tasks affect motivation and learning: Implications for struggling learners. *Reading & Writing Quarterly, 19*(1), 39.

Mills, G. E. (2010). Action research: A guide for the teacher researcher (4th ed.). Upper Saddle River, NJ: Pearson.

Mitchell, M. (1993). Situational interest: its multifaceted structure in the secondary school mathematics classroom. *Journal of Educational Psychology, 83*(3), 424–436.

Moneta, G. B., & Csikszentmihalyi, M. (1996). The effect of perceived challenges and skills on the quality of subjective experience. *Journal of Personality, 64*(2), 275.

Moos, R. H. (1979). Evaluating educational environments: Procedures, measures, findings, and policy implications. San Francisco, CA: Jossey-Bass.

Morocco, C. C., Brigham, N., & Aquilar, C. M. (2006). *Visionary middle schools: Signature practices and the power of local invention*. New York, NY: Teachers College Press.

Moses, M. S., & Nanna, M. J. (2007). The testing culture and the persistence of high-stakes testing reforms. *Education and Culture, 23*(1), 55–72.

Moss, C. M., & Brookhart, S. M. (2012). *Learning targets : helping students aim for understanding in today's lesson*. Alexandria, VA: ASCD.

Munby, H., Russell, T., & Martin, A. K. (2001). Teachers' knowledge and how it develops. In V. Richardson (Ed.), *Handbook of Research on Teaching* (4th ed., pp. 877–904). Washington, DC: American Educational Research Association.

Murray, C., & Malmgren, K. (2005). Implementing a teacher–student relationship program in a high-poverty urban school: Effects on social, emotional, and academic adjustment and lessons learned. *Journal of School Psychology, 43*(2), 137–152.

Murray, H. A. (1938). *Explorations in personality*. New York, NY: Oxford University Press.

National Comprehensive Center for Teacher Quality. (2011). *High quality professional development for all teachers*. Retrieved from, http://www.gtlcenter.org/sites/default/files/docs/HighQuality ProfessionalDevelopment.pdf.

National Partnership for Excellence and Accountability in Teaching (NPEAT). (2003). *Principles of effective professional development. Research Brief, 1*(15).

Noddings, N. (2005). *The challenge to care in schools: an alternative approach to education* (2nd ed.). New York, NY: Teachers College Press.

Noddings, N. (2006). *Critical lessons: what our schools should teach*. Cambridge, New York, NY: Cambridge University Press.

O'Connor, E., & McCartney, K. (2007). Achievement as part of an ecological model of development. *American Educational Research Journal, 44*(2), 340–369.

O'Connor, K., & Stravynski, A. (1997). Freedom and therapy: From self-liberation to self-control. *Psychotherapy, 34*(2), 144–153.

Ogbu, J. U. (2003). Black American students in an affluent suburb: A study of academic disengagement. Mawah NJ: Erlbaum Associates.

Olson, G., Duffy, S., & Mack, R. (1984). Thinking-out-loud as a method for studying real-time comprehension processes. In

D. Kieras & M. Just (Eds.), *New methods in reading comprehension research*. Hillsdale, NJ: Erlbaum.

Olsson, F. M. (2008). *New developments in the psychology of motivation*. New York, NY: Nova Biomedical Books.

Pajares, F. (1992). Teachers' beliefs and educational research: Cleaning up a messy construct. *Review of Educational Research, 62*(3), 307–332.

Pajares, F., & Urdan, T. C. (2002). *Academic motivation of adolescents*. Greenwich, CT: Information Age.

Paley, V. G. (1992). *You can't say you can't play*. Cambridge, MA: Harvard University Press.

Patrick, H., Anderman, L. H., Ryan, A. M., Edelin, K., & Midgley, C. (2001). Teachers' communication of goal orientations in four fifth-grade classrooms. *The Elementary School Journal, 102*, 35–58.

Patrick, H., Ryan, A. M., Anderman, L. H., Middleton, M., Linnenbrink, L., Hruda, L. Z., Edelin, K., Kaplan, A., & Midgley, C. (1997). *Manual for observing patterns of adaptive learning (OPAL): A protocol for classroom observations*. Ann Arbor, MI: University of Michigan.

Patrick, H., Ryan, A., & Kaplan, A. (2007). Early adolescents' perceptions of the classroom social environment, motivational beliefs, and engagement. *Journal of Educational Psychology, 99*, 83–98.

Perks, K. (2005). Dialogue folders: Creating space to engage students in conversation about their writing. In T. M. McCann, L. R. Johannessen, E. Kahn, P. Smagorinsky & M. W. Smith (Eds.), *Reflective teaching, reflective learning: How to develop critically engaged readers, writers, and speakers* (pp. 39–57). Portsmouth: Heinemann.

Perks, K., & Middleton, M. J. (2006, April). *The influence of teacher behavior on the motivation to write: A sociocultural study of motivation*. Paper presented at the 2006 Annual Meeting of the American Educational Research Association, San Francisco, CA.

Pianta, R. C., & Steinberg, M. (1992). Teacher-child relationships and the process of adjusting to school. In R. C. Pianta (Ed.), *New directions for child development* (Vol. 57, pp. 61–80). San Francisco, CA: Jossey Bass.

Pine, G. J. (2009). Teacher action research: Building knowledge democracies. Thousand Oaks, CA: SAGE.

Pintrich, P. R. (2000). Multiple goals, multiple pathways: The role of goal orientation in learning and achievement. *Journal of Educational Psychology, 92*, 544–555.

Pintrich, Paul R., & Schunk, Dale H. (2002). *Motivation in education: Theory, research, and applications* (2nd ed.). Upper Saddle River: Merrill Prentice Hall.

Pollock, J. E. (2012). *Feedback: The hinge that joins teaching and learning.* Thousand Oaks, CA: Corwin.

Reddy, R., Rhodes, J. E., & Mulhall, P. (2003). The influence of teacher support on student adjustment in the middle school years: A latent growth curve study. *Development and Pyschopathology, 15,* 119–138.

Reeve, J., Jang, H., Carrell, D., Jeon, S., & Barch, J. (2004). Enhancing students' engagement by increasing teachers' autonomy support. *Motivation and Emotion, 28*(2), 147–169.

Renninger, K. A. & Hidi, S. (2002). Interest and achievement: Developmental issues raised by a case study. In A. Wigfield & J. Eccles (Eds.), *Development of achievement motivation* (pp. 173–195). New York, NY: Academic Press.

Rosenthal, R., & Jacobson, L. (1968). Teacher expectations for the disadvantaged. *Scientific American, 218*(4), 19–23.

Roseth, C. J., Johnson, D. W., & Johnson, R. T. (2008). Promoting early adolescents' achievement and peer relationships: The effects of cooperative, competitive, and individualistic goal structures. *Psychological Bulletin, 134*(2), 223–246.

Ross, J. A. (1994). The impact of an in-service to promote cooperative learning on the stability of teacher efficacy. *Teaching and Teacher Education, 10*(4), 381–394.

Ryan, A. M., & Patrick, H. (2001). The classroom social environment and changes in adolescents' motivation and engagement during middle school. *American Educational Research Journal, 38*(2), 437–460.

Ryan, R. M., & Deci, E. L. (2000). Self-determination theory and the facilitation of intrinsic motivation, social development, and well-being. *American Psychologist, 55,* 68–78.

Ryan, R. M., & Deci, E. L. (2002). Overview of self-determination theory: An organismic dialectal perspective. In E. L. Deci & R. M. Ryan (Eds.), *Handbook of self-determination research* (pp. 2–33). Rochester, NY: University of Rochester Press.

Ryan, R. M., & Deci, E. L. (2006). Self-regulation and the problem of human autonomy: Does psychology need choice, self-determination, and will? *Journal of Personality, 74*(6), 1557–1586.

Sanders, M. G., (2003). Community involvement in school improvement: The little extra that makes a big difference. pp. 30–39. In

Epstein, et al.. (2002). *School, family, and community partnerships: Your handbook for action* (2nd ed.). Thousand Oaks, CA: Corwin Press.

Sansone, C., & Harackiewicz, J. M. (2000). *Intrinsic and extrinsic motivation: The search for optimal motivation and performance*. San Diego, CA: Academic Press.

Sarason, S. B. (1999). *Teaching as a performing art*. New York, NY: Teachers College Press.

Sawyer, R. K. (2008). Learning music from collaboration. *International Journal of Educational Research, 47*(1), 50–59.

Schon, D. (1990). *Educating the reflective practitioner*. San Francisco, CA: Jossey-Bass.

Schunk, D. H., & Pajares, F. (2005). Competence perceptions and academic functioning. In A. J. Elliot & C. S. Dweck (Eds.), *Handbook of competence and motivation* (pp. 85–104). New York, NY: The Guilford Press.

Schunk, D. H., Pintrich, P. R., & Meece, J. L. (2008). *Motivation in education* (3rd ed.). Upper Saddle River, NJ: Pearson Merrill Prentice Hall.

Sethi, S. (1998). Choice and its discontents: A new look at the role of choice in intrinsic motivation. (Ph.D. dissertation), Stanford University, Palo Alto.

Shernoff, D. J., Csikszentmihalyi, M., Schneider, B., & Shernoff, E. S. (2003). Student engagement in high school classrooms from the perspective of flow theory. *School Psychology Quarterly, 18*(2), 158–176.

Shouse, R. (1996). Academic press and sense of community: Conflict, congruence, and implications for student achievement. *Social Psychology of Education, 1*, 47–68.

Shulman, L. S. (1986). Those who understand: Knowledge growth in teaching. *Educational Researcher, 15*(2), 4–31.

Shulman, L. S. (1987). Knowledge and teaching: Foundations of the new reform. *Harvard Educational Review, 57*(1), 1–22.

Shulman, L. (1992, September-October). Ways of seeing, ways of knowing, ways of teaching, ways of learning about teaching. *Journal of Curriculum Studies, 28*, 393–396.

Sidorkin, A. (2009). *Labor of learning*. Rotterdam: Sense.

Siegel, D. (2010). *Mindsight*. New York, NY: Bantam Books.

Simmons, R. G. & Blyth, D. A. (1987). Moving into adolescence: The impact of pubertal change and social context. Hawthorne, NY: Aldine.

Slavin, R. E. (1991). *Student team learning: a practical guide to cooperative learning* (3rd ed.). Washington, DC: NEA Professional Library, National Education Association.

Slavin, R. E. (1995). *Cooperative learning: theory, research, and practice* (2nd ed.). Boston, MA: Allyn and Bacon.

Steele, C. M. (1997). A threat in the air: How stereotypes shape intellectual identity and performance. *American Psychologist, 52*(6), 613–629.

Steele, C. M., & Aronson, J. (1995). Stereotype threat and the intellectual test performance of African Americans. *Journal of Personality and Social Psychology 69*(5), 797–811.

Stefanou, C. R., Perencevich, K. C., Dicintio, M., & Turner, J. C., (2004). Supporting autonomy in the classroom: ways teachers encourage student decision making and ownership. *Educational Psychologist, 39*(2), 97–100.

Strobel, J., & van Barneveld, A. (2009). When is PBL more effective? A meta-synthesis of meta-analyses comparing PBL to conventional classrooms. *The Interdisciplinary Journal of Problem-Based Learning, 3*(1).

Swetnam, L. A. (1992). Media distortion of the teacher image. *Clearing House, 66*(1), 30–32.

Teven, J. J. (2001). The relationships among teacher characteristics and perceived caring. *Communication Education, 50*(2), 159–169.

Thomas, J. W. (2000). A review of research on project-based learning. San Rafael, CA: The Autodesk Foundation.

Thompson, B., & Mazer, J. P. (2012). College student ratings of student academic support: Frequency, importance and modes of communication. *Communication Education 58*, 433–458.

Tomlinson, C. A. (2008). The goals of differentiation. *Educational Leadership, 66*(3), 26–30.

Toshalis, E., & Nakkula, M. J. (2012). *Motivation, engagement, and student voice* (pp. 50). Boston, MA: Jobs for the Future.

Turner, J. C., Parkes, J., Cox, K. E., Meyer, D. K., Hinchman, K. A., Leu, D. J., & Kinzer, C. K. (1995). The role of optimal challenge in students' literacy engagement *Perspectives on literacy research and practice: Forty-fourth yearbook of the National Reading Conference.* (pp. 126–136). Chicago, IL, US: National Reading Conference, Inc.

Walberg, H. J., & Anderson, G. J. (1968). Classroom climate and individual learning. *Journal of Educational Psychology, 59*(6), 414–419.

Walker, A., & Leary, H. (2009). A problem-based learning meta analysis: Differences across problem types, implementation types, disciplines, and assessment levels. *Interdisciplinary Journal of Problem-based Learning, 3*(1), 12–43.

Wanzer, M. B., & McCroskey, J. C. (1998). Teacher socio-communicative style as a correlate of student affect toward teacher and course material. *Communication Education, 47*(1), 43–52.

Weiner, B. (1986). *An attributional theory of motivation and emotion.* New York, NY: Springer-Verlag.

Wentzel, K. R., Battle, A., Russell, S., & Looney, L. (2010). Social supports from teachers and peers as predictors of academic and social motivation. *Contemporary Educational Psychology, 35*, 193–202.

Wentzel, K. R., & Caldwell, K. (2006). Friendships, peer acceptance, and group membership: Relations to academic achievement in middle school. *Child Development, 68*(6), 1198–1209.

Wigfield, A., & Eccles, J. S. (2000). Expectancy-value theory of achievement motivation. *Contemporary Educational Psychology, 25*, 68–81.

Wigfield, A., Eccles, J. S., & Rodriguez, D. (1998). The development of children's motivation in school contexts. *Review of Research in Education, 23*, 73–118.

Wigfield, A., & Eccles, J. S. (2002). *Development of achievement motivation.* San Diego, CA: Academic Press.

Wiggins, G., & McTighe, J. (2008). Put understanding first. *Educational Leadership, 65*(8), 36.

Wilson, B. L., & Corbett, H. D. (2001). Listening to urban kids: School reform and the teachers they want. New York, NY: State University of New York Press.

Wilson, G. B. (2006). Breaking through barriers to boys' achievement: developing a caring masculinity. London, England: Network Continuum Education.

Wolfgang, C. (2005). Solving discipline and classroom management problems: Methods and models for today's teachers (6th ed.). Hoboken, NJ: John Wiley & Sons.

Woolfolk A. E., & Hoy, W. K. (2004). The educational psychology of teacher efficacy. *Educational Psychology Review, 16*, 153–176. Woolfolk, A. E., & Hoy, W. K., (1990). Prospective teachers' sense of efficacy and beliefs about control, *Journal of Educational Psychology, 82*, 81–91.

Yazzie-Mintz, E. (2010). Charting the path from engagement to achievement: A report on the 2009 high school survey of student engagement. Retrieved from, http://ceep.indiana.edu/hssse/images/HSSSE_2010_Report.pdf.

Zimmer-Gembeck, M. J., & Locke, E. M. (2007). The socialization of adolescent coping: Relationships at home and school. *Journal of Adolescence, 30*, 1–16.

Zimmerman, B. J. (1990). Self-regulated learning and academic achievement: An overview. *Educational Psychologist, 25*(1), 3–17.

Index

CORWIN
A SAGE Company

The Corwin logo—a raven striding across an open book—represents the union of courage and learning. Corwin is committed to improving education for all learners by publishing books and other professional development resources for those serving the field of PreK–12 education. By providing practical, hands-on materials, Corwin continues to carry out the promise of its motto: **"Helping Educators Do Their Work Better."**